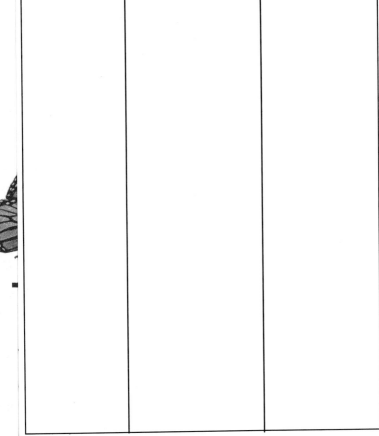

This book is due for return on or before
the last date shown below

Olivier van Duuren

"We are in the midst of unprecedented transformation of the world as we know it. As people and companies seek to navigate the pace of change, look to *The Dualarity* – an exceptional tool for those seeking guidance on how to lead your life, maximize your business, and harness innovation for good."

Carolyn Everson, Vice President, Global Marketing Solutions, Facebook

"Transformation risks being abused as a new buzzword. Change can still be forced. Transformation cannot be forced. Transformation is the result of a profound and honest process between employees, leaders and managers. Energy, joy, honesty, courage and humility are engaging human ingredients to make transformational dynamics possible. This book is a reliable guide to implement an organic and sustainable transformational culture. A caterpillar cannot be forced to become a butterfly. Olivier helps you to understand this process."

André Pelgrims, Change architect and director, Taking Wing

"Olivier's writing and insight are easy to understand and digest. The reason; he's lived the trends he is speaking about. He has seen firsthand the methods that work and the bad habits that don't. *The Dualarity* is a roadmap to the digital transformation both professionally and personally."

Bob Bejan, Global Communications Strategy, Microsoft

"The concept of *The Dualarity* is interesting: in this fast changing world, we all try to align our personal values and maturities to those of the organizations we work for. Olivier succeeds in well articulating the tensions of this journey, and offers a powerful toolkit for self-reflection."

Peter Vander Auwera, co-founder, Innotribe and SWIFT International

"Olivier has written an excellent book on how people and organizations can transform themselves during a period of unprecedented disruption that has only just started. The book itself not only explains the Dualarity, it also practices it by successfully balancing inspirational examples with very pragmatic frameworks and models. You will walk away from the book energized and ready to apply Dualarity principles to yourself and your organization."

Norm Johnston, Global Chief Strategy & Digital Officer,
Mindshare, author of *Adaptive Marketing*

"We don't live in an era of changes, but in the change of eras. The world around us is changing rapidly. As a human being, entrepreneur, business person, employer or employee, we have two options: deal with the changes or get left behind. *The Dualarity* helps you not only to see the transformations in the world, businesses and on a personal level, but also how you can cope with them. Olivier shows the way to see opportunities in change. He guides us in a practical way to become more mindful about the impact of transformations."

Karel Van Eetvelt, CEO of UNIZO Flemish Union
of entrepreneurs, SMEs and free professions

"I really enjoyed the fresh perspectives Olivier brings to dealing with extreme change in business. *The Dualarity* is a must read for those who embrace the concepts of rapid iteration and paradox in the digital age."

Darren Huston, CEO & Founder, BlackPines Global Advisors,
and former CEO, Priceline/Booking.com

"Olivier provides an insightful view on how the digital era affects our society. Singularity implies that we are just at the beginning of a makeover journey of our society, companies and ourselves. *The Dualarity* makes the counterintuitive case that for all the digital change, we need to work on transforming ourselves. Olivier helps you understand your current position in the cycle of your life and provides a powerful model for self-development. It is the next chapter in your search for happiness. Only then can you hope to empower other professionals or managers in transforming the organisation. *The Dualarity* is a timely book: personal balance is a condition of sustainable business success."

Duco Sickinghe, Managing Partner, Fortino, and former CEO, Telenet

"How do you grow when surviving is already a challenge? How do you transform when performing is a fulltime job? Olivier helps you find the energy and insights to not only to successfully undertake this journey but actually enjoy it too. As an organisation, a team and, even more important, as an individual. Inspiring cases and tips from a business leader who rode the waves of transformation himself."

Sven Mastbooms, futurist at Kindred Spirits

"It's 2045 and computer power exceeds human power and starts generating its own intelligence. Technology is now evolving at a faster rate than an organisation can adapt. Machines are more intelligent than people. This is singularity. The fear is people become redundant, dispensable and replaceable. Not true says digital visionary and thought leader, Olivier Van Duüren. In his thought provoking and inspiring book, *The Dualarity*, he argues that the digital future will be more about the partnership between technology and transformation – personal and professional. Rather than a balancing act he predicts it will be more like complementing opposites – yin and yang – performing and transforming, personal and business. This is a challenging, fascinating and refreshing read."

Daniel Priestley, entrepreneur, international speaker and best-selling author of *Key Person of Influence* and *The Entrepreneur Revolution*

"The Dualarity is a highly practical approach to becoming more mindful on how the Digital Transformation is impacting all of us, both professionally as well as in our personal lives. A must-read to better understand the dynamics of this transformation, to avoid being stuck in the present and to create more mental space and clarity."

Stijn Nauwelaerts, General Manager HR,
Microsoft Global Sales, Marketing and Operations

"This book gives you the opportunity to surf on the extraordinary experience of Olivier. To those willing to put the consumer at heart, people as the soul and digital as the oxygen in their organization, it is a great tool for dealing with the increasing complexity of the digital reality we all live in."

Wouter Quartier, Strategy Manager, VRT Belgian broadcaster

"With *The Dualarity,* Olivier synthesizes decades of experience working globally as a leader in the digital revolution. Employing compelling data, the insightful observations of other business innovators and real-time corporate situations to illuminate his conclusions, this nicely paced book should motivate you to evaluate where you stand in relation to digital transformation, and then get you to move, and keep moving. Olivier summarizes succinctly and accurately: 'If we want to transform our businesses, we start by transforming ourselves.'"

Whitney Johnson, Thinkers50, World's Most Influential
Management Thinkers, author of critically-acclaimed
Disrupt Yourself: Putting the Power of Disruptive Innovation to Work

REΞTHINK PRESS

First published in Great Britain 2016
by Rethink Press (www.rethinkpress.com)

I dedicate this book to all of you around the globe who are living in the Dualarity and are looking to find balance in your personal and business transformation. I hope *The Dualarity* will help you find it.

Table Of Contents

Preface – The Tintin Reporter

I am truly excited, honoured and humbled by the idea that you are reading my book. I hope you enjoy the Dualarity spirit, the field journalism and the concept I've outlined.

Being a Belgian in heart and soul, while writing the book I have channelled the character Tintin, the fictional hero of *The Adventures of Tintin* in the comic series by Belgian cartoonist Hergé. Tintin is a reporter, journalist and adventurer who travels around the world. Through his investigative reporting, quick-thinking and all-round good nature, Tintin is always able to solve the mystery and complete the adventure. I am a slightly ageing Tintin, but I honour his spirit of discovery, learning and seeing the world as his home. I am enjoying a journey full of adventures and colourful encounters, soft and hard life learnings, travel and self-development, passion and friendships, light and darkness, and failures and successes.

My adventure started on 14 August 1994 when I joined Microsoft. I had no idea how powerful that decision would be or how it would flavour my future life. So many experiences, so much personal growth. I loved the passion, the possibilities, the people, the persistence and the energy. I was proud to be part of something that is shaping the future world. Since 2014 Microsoft has wanted to empower every person and every organisation on the planet to achieve more, a full transformation under CEO Satya Nadella's inspiring and refreshing leadership, always fully in with his heart and soul.

'I love this company,' were the famous four words said by Steve Ballmer, former CEO of Microsoft, and there hasn't been a CEO more outrageously and sincerely enthusiastic about his company than Steve. I must say I felt the same during most of my twenty-two years with Microsoft. My grown up kids have only known me there; they even believed, when they were young, that I *was* Microsoft. I was fortunate to be supported by my amazing wife Heidi who has been with me every step of the journey around the rock of life. I made a lot of friends, learned so much, and have been constantly amazed by Microsoft's ability to adapt, learn from its failures, accelerate successes and reinvent itself.

During my international roles and travel I discovered many beautiful places, people and cultures from around the globe before coming back to my home country in 2015. In November 2015, I decided I had to move on to follow my passion for transformation in all its senses and to share it with others. I decided to resign from my last role as COO-CMO of Microsoft Belux after twenty-two years of service.

I didn't have a Plan B when I resigned, so I worked for Microsoft on digital transformation for six more months until the end of June 2016. This vacuum gave me time to decide what I wanted to do, and while many thought leaving my very attractive role without having a Plan B to be a mistake, a jump into the dark unknown, I felt like I was jumping into the light. After so many years I was ready to cut the umbilical cord with Microsoft. I followed my passion, made room for something to grow while ending an era, and gave birth to The Dualarity. I also wrote this book, which has been in the making for twenty-two years.

Very early on in my career I realised, through my international roles, the global and local change projects, the intensive travel around the world and meeting people, that I was leading the curve of transformation. Trying to solve global challenges – multiple challenges at the same time, seeing things others couldn't see, and connecting the dots to make more sense. Determining new ways of working. Looking to bridge people with business; getting energised by working with people from around the world. Due to the nature of my evolving roles, my passion for people and for the future, I saw patterns around how to succeed where wellbeing was centre stage, and more importantly, I learned how to *fail successfully* in my personal and business transformation – I've had many successes but learned far more from my failures. I learned fast and I enjoyed the rollercoaster ride.

I thought deeply about what it means to transform and perform at the same time – to transform yourself so you can transform others – and I came up with a concept: The Dualarity. A dualarity is a technological singularity with a duality, which of course makes no sense, so I need to elaborate – explain and uncover, like all good investigative reporters.

A technological singularity is a point where computing power exceeds human power. Duality is zeros and ones, left and right, heads and tails, transforming and performing – two states that are opposites and complementary. Dualarity is where the dual world meets the singularity – where two can coincide and thrive in a technological world full of possibilities.

In the book I will introduce you to the Dualarity Quadrant, and I'll take you through that journey in my roles as a reporter from the outside and an adventurer who has lived inside the Dualarity, reflecting on the journey and sharing the learnings. The Dualarity Quadrant shows how you can be scared, injured, healthy or mature, and how you can move from one quadrant to another. This movement, this pendulum, is when you are truly living in the Dualarity. Each Dualarity stage reflects a certain moment in time, and you'll change multiple times, both as a person and as a business. It's a very simple model, easy to map yourself, your team or your business in the quadrants. Finding alignment between your individual place and where your organisation is on the quadrant is the core of the Dualarity.

The 'Seeing' part of the book helps you make sense of what is happening around you, which is critical. Too many remain ignorant on purpose, from lack of time or by accident. In the 'Energising' section of the book I help you find the energy to do something about what you've seen – this is a business book with tools you can choose from to help you in your own journey. The Dualarity tools and the Fitness Test will help you discover the status of your company and yourself by showing what quadrant you're in and how you can move from one quadrant to another. As companies are composed of individuals, it is important to map yourself in the Dualarity before you map others and your business.

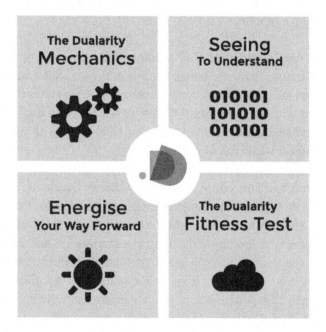

The book goes beyond personal memories as it combines field journalism, my experiences, my personal transformation, my life moments and business learnings with a mix of world observations and seeing in this digital age. It is a fast moving subject area, and my aim is to make it accessible to all levels.

I hope you'll be able to say, 'I read it, I see, I understand, I tested myself, I changed, I got re-energised as an entrepreneur and as a person.'

It is all about human business, a dualarity of being first human and then worker; of performing while transforming in this digital revolution.

Learn to fly, tap into the energy of your personal and business transformation, and become a butterfly.

Introduction

The world has changed; we live in a disrupted society and industry. During the past few years we have seen more changes than any generation before – changes in the very nature and fabric of our home environment; in the way we work and play; the way we communicate with our families, our children, our employees, our colleagues and friends. Changes in the way we converse as citizens with our governments and the way we evaluate and share our views on the products and services of our preferred brands. The pace of change is faster than ever and not showing any signs of slowing down.

The mass adoption of digital innovations like artificial intelligence, robotics and wearables, along with the democratisation of technology with accessible, affordable and adaptable products, and the evolutions in biological and energy spheres with genetically editable organisms, neuro-technical enhancement and electric cars, fosters a society and industry geared towards the fast and the furious – a world where your mobile has morphed into the remote control of your digital life. These trends are dominating the discussions, their combined effect is even greater than their individual impact, and we need to think deeply about the future to remain successful, happy and productive as individuals and as organisations.

Ninety per cent of start-ups launch and are gone before they can scale to the $1billion 'unicorn' status. Large companies disappear, being acquired, merged or dissolved. Half a century ago, the life expectancy of Fortune 500 companies was around seventy-five years; now it's less than fifteen years and declining even further. Job roles and hierarchies are created and extinguished in a moment in virtual conference calls across time zones and international borders, while others not only survive, but positively thrive in this digital world, transforming their businesses, taking advantage of digital innovations, and realising potential in their teams and themselves.

So, how do you transform your organisation from an enterprise that engages in digital to a digital enterprise? This is no small challenge for companies with a long history, shareholders around the globe, thousands of employees and customers, assets worth millions, sometimes billions, and established business models. These incumbent companies often lack the agility, speed and flexibility of the start-ups and find it difficult to reimagine parts of or their whole business. Our future holds great opportunity, but new risks at the same time.

Against the backdrop of these innovations and disruptions, the human element is often overlooked. We're even shifting our understanding of what it means to be human with the rise of robots, the humanoids. It has led to disruptions in our personal and professional lives – if we want to lead others, we need to start by leading ourselves. If we want to transform our businesses, we start by transforming ourselves.

Our world is becoming a Dualarity, a technologically advanced world of dualities: the digital haves and have nots; the believers and the non-believers; the excited and the scared; the unnecessary conflict between work and life; the changing dynamics between creators and consumers, incumbents and entrepreneurs; opportunities to lead and the wisdom to be led; living with disharmony while searching for harmony; aiming to perform while you transform.

We need Dualarity heroes: people who are able to see beyond artificial barriers, who have a great perspective on the future, enthusiasm and a strong desire to learn and, more importantly, impart their learning. They make sense and see what others don't see, going beyond a world driven by power and profit to one that encourages mental and physical health, and a society that balances having with being. Dualarity heroes understand they can't go on the journey alone. They don't just need people sharing the disruption that is upon them, they need action to take this challenge to heart. Be the Jedi of the Dualarity. Show others the way, become a master in digital seeing and get energised by the ideas from the Dualarity principles and toolbox so you can give light in the darkness.

The heart and soul of organisations, their customers and employees, are dragged along with the disruptions, sometimes scared, often confused, frequently apprehensive. You, as a leader of a team or part of a company, can help bring the heart and soul along on the digital journey – a journey that gives much needed (digital) oxygen for the company and for yourself; a journey that gives colour to your life and can enable future success.

By seeing the opportunities, creating environments for safe growth, and energising your colleagues to be part of the Dualarity, you can lead people to perform and transform at the same time. You can lead them forward into the Dualarity. If you don't want to get Uberised, Amazonised or Netflixed but want to remain competitive, you will need to transform yourself before you can transform others. It is time to act. Do it with passion and keep it burning. Ride the waves of your transformation. With the right energy and the ability to see, to connect the zeros and ones, you will be able to go beyond survival. You will thrive in your journey.

To be or not to be in The Dualarity.

Olivier Van Duüren

The Lexicon Of The Dualarity

Dualarity: a technological singularity with a duality. Dualarity is recognising that the singularity will come in twos: performing and transforming, personal and business transformation, success and failure, transform yourself before you transform others, thinking and doing, healthy and mature, incumbents and disruptors, old and new, mental and physical, technology and humans, work and life.

Technological singularity: where computing power exceeds human power and starts developing its own intelligence.

Dualarity pendulum: when you are in the Dualarity you can move like a pendulum between being mature, more performing, and healthy, more transforming.

Dualarity Quadrant: the four quadrants of the Dualarity are scared, injured, healthy and mature.

Dualarity hero: people who are able to move like a pendulum between healthy and mature at different moments in time. They are able to find balance in performing and transforming – balance in personal and business transformation.

Incumbents: established, more traditional businesses, or often older people in current roles who are trying (or not trying) to embrace the new fast-paced digital world. Sometimes referred to as legacy.

Digital immigrants: newcomers to digital, often the older generation.

Digital natives: people who use technology as part of their normal lives, some because they were born with it. Often the millennial generation.

Disruption: shake up, change, evolve, disturb, agitate, cause a commotion or distortion, upset – in the context of personal and business disruption driven by supply and demand drivers (consumer, digital, demographical). For example, as climate disruption, like an earthquake, is used in the weather context, technology disruption is in the context of digital innovation.

Opposite to disruption: calm, method, order, organisation, systems – sounds familiar as basic foundation to incumbents or traditional businesses.

Seeing: our ability to observe, understand and make sense of digital and its implication on our society, industry and ourselves. We can see or be blind.

Energy: what we need to manage and improve to keep moving forwards. What we need to cope with to embrace what we see. Energy can be high or low.

Digital transformation: transforming a business driven by a technological and/or business model innovation into a digital business impacting the foundational elements of your business. The foundation of digital transformation is three connected ingredients: the heart, soul and oxygen of the company, all aligned to the overarching why and what.

The heart of your business is your customers.
The soul of your business is your people.
The oxygen for your business is digital.

The why of a company: the purpose, cause, or belief that inspires you to do what you do. Why is your company doing what it does?

The what of a company: what you want to achieve, your long term objectives.

5

The Dualarity Of Performing While Transforming In The Digital World

Failure and invention are inseparable twins.

Jeff Bezos, CEO Amazon

Most incumbents, established companies and individuals, struggle when challenged to respond to new entrants in their existing markets. They frequently fail to respond or respond late to new market opportunities and disruptive market creators. Their existing performing businesses are mostly profitable; they're doing well, and chasing new entrants and markets can often be less profitable with higher risks.

Less profitable or unprofitable companies are also being disrupted, and it's not being profitable that keeps companies from innovating. Change goes against the natural impulse of a business, which is to carry on doing what works, what delivers results, keeping busy with the short term performance. Many businesses have neither the time nor the strategic desire to transform at the same time. Some fail to recognise that what's happening outside may affect them. In essence, most people don't like change and will resist.

The most disrupted industries suffer from low barriers to entry leading to more agile competition. They are populated with large, historical businesses that generate the vast majority of revenue and often profit, and these businesses are not fluid or agile enough to meet with the changing pace of technology. The size of a business was once a competitive advantage, allowing companies to compete globally and work with other large companies. Now, size is becoming a liability as businesses that once dominated the market are struggling to keep up with young, nimble and flexible start-ups, who are using digital to unlock opportunity and as their platform to grow. On the other hand, many of the start-ups are still in a pre-start-up phase: they don't have an extensive network, lack business experience and will fail to reach profitability and scale. They are disrupting while not making money, but bringing new value that customers demand. So, incumbents and start-ups alike need to find the balance between meeting increasing customer demand and long term profitability. A perfect marriage.

> Many leaders of big organizations, I think, don't believe that change is possible. But if you look at history, things do change, and if your business is static, you're likely to have issues.
>
> **Larry Page, co-founder of Google**

Now is the moment for organisations to re-assess their customer relationships, their talent assets, their resource allocation, their market offerings and the competitive landscape they are playing in. It is a moment where the global economic world is rebooting, powered by a new, open operating system – a new reality where incumbents need to understand the long-term implications for their business and start-ups need to create a plan for profitability and scale.

Most executives are probably aware of the bigger trends; they're reading articles from the experts or futurologists, following the change makers, but the main challenge is how they can move their established organisation from seeing to taking action while judging how radical the shift will be. Over the years they've probably overestimated the speed of change and underestimated the impact.

Digital reshapes whole industries with unlimited, accessible computing capacity and real-time analytics, allowing enterprises to access new insights and build systems of intelligence like never before. Companies are making transformational changes in how they innovate their business, how their employees work, and how they engage with customers. They need to, or are, changing from an enterprise using digital to a digital enterprise, with a digital-first mindset. As many parts of an industry or business mature, the original value evaporates as it becomes more commoditised, and it needs to find new sources of value. This is where digital can act as the oxygen for a business; this is where digital comes into play.

> Digital business is the creation of new business designs by blurring the digital and physical worlds. It promises to usher in an unprecedented convergence of people, business and things that disrupts existing business models.
>
> Gartner, an American research and advisory firm providing information technology related insights to businesses.

Innovation and technology are evolving on an exponential curve, with predictions that the growth will continue and in a few decades the power of all computers will exceed that of human brains. This point, where computing power exceeds human power and starts developing its own intelligence, where it's possible to build a machine that is more intelligent than humans, is the technological singularity. The predicted dates for the singularity are mostly around 2045.

At the **technological singularity,** artificially intelligent machines would be capable, by auto self-learning and improvement, of an intelligence surpassing all current human understanding – a super-intelligence[1] that may be impossible for a human to comprehend. Some people believe it may be unpredictable or even unfathomable to human intelligence.

Brian Solis, author of *What's the Future of Business,* among other titles, claims that digital Darwinism is the phenomenon when technology and society evolve faster than an organisation can adapt:

If you do not adapt, you will fall to digital Darwinism. You are competing as much for relevance as you are market share. By re-imagining your company's direction and how it works, technology (and people) become part of the solution instead of the problem. This increases revenue, cuts costs and improves competitive advantages.

It's like reaching the singularity for a company. When looking at what might be possible in the digital future, we need our world to respond with a Dualarity. A Dualarity is a technological singularity with a duality.[2]

Dualarity is recognising that the singularity will come in twos: performing and transforming, personal and business transformation, success and failure, transform yourself before you transform others, thinking and doing, healthy and mature, incumbents and disruptors, old and new, mental and physical, technology and humans, work and life. In addition, even if society adapts, technology evolves and your business is agile enough to make the grade, you as an individual need to join the journey. The individual as part of society, part of the organisation, needs to align and balance. The transformation needs to happen at the personal level before it can transform business. This is a Dualarity.

Many of the things we do, at work or at home, are about making our lives easier. Save me time! Save me money! Make everything easier! Creating beautiful things and producing art are ways to express ourselves, enhancing a personal balance, improving business and personal health. Everybody seeks to have this ease, balance beyond their primary needs as a human being.

Nigel Kershaw, *Big Issue* Executive Chairman, says, 'Tech puts power into people's hands and has the potential to change both attitudes and lives.' The impact on society of the changes we are seeing now will be much bigger than the impact on industry. We tend to underestimate the impact digital will have on the way we live, where we live and with whom we live.

> **Tintin Snack: technology is like gravity.** I was talking with my best friend, explaining my enthusiasm for technology. He doesn't like technology very much in general; he's probably afraid of it and has some nostalgia for the past. After an animated discussion, I said to him, 'You can argue. You can agree or disagree, but you will not stop it. You can say you don't believe in it. You can fight it. It doesn't matter whether you believe in technology, it will act on you and your life, just like gravity.' Today, digital is already like gravity. It is everywhere in our lives from renting a car to going on holiday, doing grocery shopping, streaming movies, at retirement homes, reporting taxes, when doing sports.

Even non-believers, those who don't want to use technology or don't think technology can help them, are likely to end up coming to the middle, coming closer to the believers. The believers will need to meet them on middle ground and lead them. The future reality will find its balance somewhere in the middle, but even that will go far beyond today's imagination. The believers and non-believers are a Dualarity – without one we cannot have the other. The middle point is where we have balance. If we want to remove the fear, we need to create trust. Can we trust technology? How do we make sure that there's trust? Trust will probably be the single most important challenge as we move ahead, for both believers and non-believers.

Valerie Beaulieu, GM Small & Medium Business Microsoft Asia, shared the following with me:

> The person who influenced me a lot relative to technology adoption was my grandfather. He told me that when he was a boy, people were dreading the development of a power plant on the river nearby, fearing flood, fires, etc. Who today would fear electricity? It's definitely part of our lives.

If you want to influence and lead others, first you need to lead yourself. Without personal transformation you cannot lead business transformation. Transformation has to start with you.

> Disrupting yourselves is secret to breaking into a new field. Never settling for less and achieving more.
>
> **Whitney Johnson, *Disrupt Yourself:***
> ***Putting the power of disruptive innovation to work***

When one changes, others are destined to change as a consequence. If you change as an individual, your business will also change, and hopefully for the better. It's a Dualarity, and part of the ecology of change.

Racing out as an individual or business and investing in technology is not the answer. The change must come from within; the leadership, culture, mindset, behaviours are the drivers of balance. From these you will perform and transform. Technology alone will not set you apart in the future. You might need to become a software company, where software and technology will be in everything you do: your devices, your services, running your metrics, measuring your life. This is a Dualarity of technology and human change. We cannot have one without the other.

Leaving the problem to the next generation, waiting for the millennials to come along to fix your technology imbalance (assuming that by 2025 50% of the working population will be millennials) will not be a good solution. Gareth Ellis-Williams, Head of digital at Prostate Cancer UK, says, 'Just relying on a generational shift will take a long time. We can't wait that long.' It's not about which generational group, X, Y or Z, that you belong to determining your mindset; it's about infusing the right mindset and not waiting for it to appear. We need to act now. We owe it to our kids, ourselves, our society and our businesses.

> It's time to understand it – and not as a curiosity or an entry in the annals of technology or business but as an integral part of our humanity, as the latest and most powerful extension and expression of the project of being human.
>
> **Virginia Heffernan,** *Magic and Loss: The Internet as Art*

The Heart, The Soul And The Oxygen Of An Organisation

And the only way to do great work is to love what you do. If you haven't found it yet, keep looking. Don't settle. Follow your heart, your intuition.

Steve Jobs, Stanford University commencement speech

What defines us, what we need to live, our heart, our soul and oxygen, can be mapped by how we view business and organisations. The same three pillars form the foundation for your business: put the customer at the heart, see digital as the oxygen and value people as the soul. These need to go hand-in-hand with the company's overarching why – your purpose, your cause, what you believe and for whom – and the what – proof, the result, what you do. First you must determine your why and what before you craft your heart, soul and oxygen pillars.

Transforming while performing is a true balancing act, challenging companies of all sizes in this digital revolution powered by new technologies crossing the physical, digital and biological world. How do you find the right balance between performing – delivering on the short-term commitments of your core products and services, such as scorecard, P&L, market share – and transforming – the long-term belief in your future and the power to adapt and lead? You do this by looking at the three interconnected pillars for your organisation: heart, soul and oxygen.

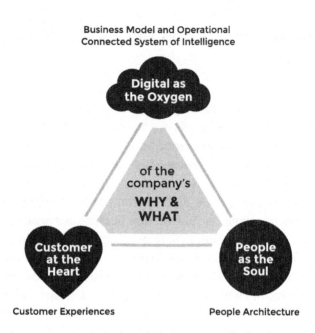

There are three fundamental questions in making digital transformation real. How do you:

1 Engage your customers, deliver and enhance the end to end customer experience for products and services, and put **the customer at the heart**? How do you innovate your products to deliver a great and frictionless experience? This is your business to customer strategy

2 Transform your business, such as your business model, operations, process, offerings and products, by embracing innovation to be more responsive, efficient, fluid, agile and predictive? How do you make **digital the oxygen of your company**? This is your business to business strategy

3 Empower your employees and organise yourself in the most productive way, reward cross-group collaboration, develop the right skills and mindsets, and attract and retain the right talent by having **people as the soul**? This is your business to employee strategy.

And they have to be aligned to the why and the what of your business. We'll talk more about this later when we discover what Simon Sinek has written about the why in his *Start With Why*.

The real question will be: how can you accelerate, scale and mainstream digital transformation in your organisation? And it has to be more than new words with old instruments. No one has really cracked it yet and there is probably no single formula, but what I will do in this next section is share my views and my learnings to act as a guide for you and your business so you can thrive in this fast-paced world.

An MIT Massachusetts Institute of Technology study on digital transformation has shown the companies that have digitally transformed are 26% more profitable than their average industry competitors:[3]

> The CEO of tomorrow operates the business with real-time comprehensive information and instant global communications, and understands what is happening as it is happening and acts accordingly.

And this transformation is not just about technology, innovation and science; it's about people, culture, behaviours, passion and mindsets.

> A good entrepreneur finds the good wave and avoids the negative undercurrent.
>
> **Geert Noels, founder of Econopolis**

We'll look a little more at these three pillars in the 'Dualarity Toolbox' section, where I'll show how you can build a digital business that transforms while performing.

The Dualarity Mechanics

The Dualarity
Mechanics

We first develop the Ego, then encounter the Soul, and finally give birth to a unique sense of Self.

Carol S. Pearson, author *Awakening the Heroes Within: Twelve archetypes to help us find ourselves and transform our world*

Let's look at the Dualarity archetypes, and how you can map yourself and your business.

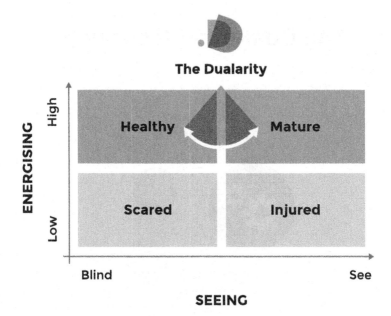

Depending on where you are as a person, as a business or the current state of your mind, you will fall into one of these boxes. You will move multiple times in a lifetime around the boxes. If you're open to see, you can energise yourself to move and elevate yourself above the centre line: the average of all the stages of your life as an individual and your business life – the good states or positive states, the bad states or negative states. You could spend your whole life injured or scared, or perhaps a portion of your life has been healthy, or mature. It's the average that counts. You will move from one stage to another. As an individual this change might occur daily (one day you feel healthy, the next scared, or some people might even change their moods by the hour), but a company or team might take more time to move from one quadrant to another.

There are four quadrants. You as an individual and/or your organisation may be at this moment in time:

1 Scared – you have limited visibility on what's happening in the world around you, and you have low energy. You are blind and scared to move

2 Injured – you have seen the world and may have been injured while attempting to develop within it. You may have had a bad experience, or you may be able to see all the problems and opportunities but lack the energy to move and take advantage of the future. You are wounded but can recover with the right energy and actions

3 Healthy – you have abundant energy. You have not experienced it all, your view may be limited, but you have enthusiasm and energy for the future. You are willing to take risks. You may hit problems from lack of vision or experience, like everyone does, but you bounce back up with energy. You learn fast and move on. This is a very nurturing quadrant to be in, often a place where you find young children or start-ups, and some large companies can be in this stage. It may be that a part of your business sits or need to sit in here

4 Mature – you have plenty of visibility on the world, you see and you have energy to keep going forward. You have been through a few wars and have wisdom; you know because you have experienced it. You have reached the stage of maturity in your life or business path.

Being in one quadrant reflects just a certain moment in time, and you'll change often. It is not a constant state you are in; you fluctuate – both as a person and as a business.

There is also the Dualarity pendulum, balancing between healthy and mature. This is a moving point where you continuously improve, always look to see more. It is the balance, the ability to perform and transform where you switch between healthy and mature. The trick, the key to living in the Dualarity, is being able to see where you are now and what you need to do to move, transform and balance. You have to detect in your organisation and around you in your personal or business life in which quadrant you are right now.

Let's think about the diagram from a business perspective. Some mature incumbents are very successful at business, they may have been profitable for many years, but if they don't see what's coming next, they won't be able to move into the Dualarity point, the pendulum, where they can transform. They need to become healthy again, learn new things, be brave, not knowing exactly where this will lead as they possibly enter a new market or launch a new product. They need to take more risks, once more becoming entrepreneurial.

Many non-technological incumbents[4] are increasingly betting on technology companies to fuel their growth and digital transformation by doing targeted acquisitions, such as Walmart buying Kosmix, Nordstrom buying HauteLook, Disney buying Hulu, or by making select investments in technology, such as JP Morgan investing in Prosper Marketplace and Visa in Square.

When you are in the Dualarity you can move like a pendulum between being mature and healthy – balancing. During the day, week, month, year or the process you'll be in the healthy quadrant, more transforming, and then you'll be mature, more performing. Dualarity heroes find the right balance between healthy and mature at different moments in time.

As a business, one day you may find yourself in the injured quadrant. You see some of what is happening around you, but you don't have the energy to do something with it or to fight and take action. You are wounded by the changes. There is hope – you can still become healthy or mature again. You will need to find a coalition of the willing around you who have energy to move and revive yourself. If not, you might end up in the scared quadrant.

Businesses with low energy and blind to the opportunities are scared. They often end up as failed businesses or being taken over. They hold on to the past, looking behind them at their best days, wishing the world hadn't changed. People in the scared quadrant, who don't see any more and are not energised to move, tend to fall into depression or burn out.

It's a simple model and it's very easy to map yourself, your team or your business in the quadrant. Finding alignment between your individual place and where your organisation fits on the quadrant is the core of the Dualarity. Of course, there's another dualarity within the model; it's not a two-dimensional static model. The Dualarity between you as an individual and you as a leader in an organisation can also be mapped. While you may be able to see and have great energy, if you are working in an organisation where there's little visibility or energy, on the one hand you may be able to help the organisation see and have energy too, or you may feel frustrated and hold back. Leaving the company might be the price you pay.

So, you can map businesses and people to see the fit. Go to the 'Dualarity Fitness Test' section to see how to test and map yourself and your business to discover whether there's harmony or disharmony. Discover the overlay of yourself and your business with our simple tests so you can work out how to move forwards.

Now, let's look at the dynamics of the different archetypes in the Dualarity model in more detail.

Dynamics Of The Dualarity Archetypes

Make your interactions with people transformational, not just transactional.

Patti Smith, American singer-songwriter, poet, and visual artist

Let's look in some detail at the dynamics of the Dualarity archetypes, how they interact, how you can move from one quadrant to another, what companies we might see in each quadrant and how to identify where you are today.

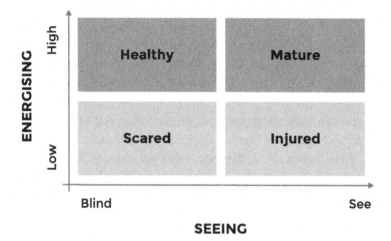

Scared

The low energy and blind quadrants are where we find scared businesses and people. Scared is about being insecure, in survival mode, paralysed, searching around in the dark. The degree of change is so high that scared people don't see it any more; they are unable to understand the opportunities and just see the threats. Often they are burned out, suffering from depression. The world around them has changed, they hold on to the past and they can't see the light at the end of the tunnel. They might have tried to battle, but it took all their energy and they didn't succeed.

A scared company doesn't see the value of digital and how to use it to its benefit. It has weak or the wrong leadership and does not put the customer at the heart; it is an inside-out company. Its people are demotivated and it needs to let them go. It doesn't know why it does what it does or what it wants to achieve.

Who fits in the scared quadrant? Let us take a look at the former rulers of the mobile world: Blackberry, Motorola and Nokia. They all moved from being very healthy and mature to injured and ended up in the scared quadrant, even though Blackberry is still fighting to reclaim its place.

Setting the scene. Before 2007, the mobile market was mainly ruled by those three giants. BlackBerry Inc., a wireless handheld devices and services company, formerly known as Research in Motion Limited (RIM), based in the US, was considered one of the major smartphone vendors in the world, differentiating their offer with secure communications and mobile productivity through their advanced email. Celebrities, captains of industry, global leaders and consumers used a blackberry at the time.

Motorola Inc. was a multinational telecommunications company based in the US. Its handset division was seen as a pioneer in cellular telephones.

Nokia, created in 1865 and based in Finland, transformed from a rubber boots maker to the leader in the world of mobile phones. In 2005 Nokia sold its billionth phone.

What happened? Two juggernauts, new kids on the block, launched new phone experiences, not just products. Apple flipped the mobile industry upside down by introducing the iPhone in 2007, and Google launched an open platform, Android, one year later enabling every smartphone manufacturer to put and sell Android on their phones. When Apple launched, everyone downplayed this innovative mobile experience emerging from Steve Jobs's obsession with empowering people through amazing experiences. Steve Ballmer from Microsoft even said, 'There's no chance that the iPhone is going to get any significant market share. No chance', and former RIM senior leaders said it was just a plaything, convinced that people only wanted to do work. They all used their own framework of reference.

In 2013, BlackBerry hired a new CEO, John S. Chen, and rejected proposals from several technology companies. Chen said, 'We are committed to reclaiming our success.' In September 2013, at its peak, there were 85 million BlackBerry subscribers worldwide, but this dropped down to 23 million in March 2016. John Chen is now charged with turning this around.

Motorola, after a loss of $4.3 billion between 2007 to 2009, was divided in 2011 into two independent public companies called Motorola Mobility and Motorola Solutions. Google bought Motorola Mobility for $12.5B for their patents, and sold it again for $2.9B in 2014 to the Chinese hardware company Lenovo.

Nokia, once a source of national pride for Finns, entered in 2011 into a deal with Microsoft to use its Windows Phone platform exclusively on future smartphones. In 2014 Nokia's mobile phone business was bought by Microsoft for $7.17 billion dollars, and in 2016 Microsoft announced the sale of the Nokia-branded phone division to FIH Mobile, a division of Foxconn, and HMD, a company in Finland, for $350 million.

All three companies saw massive lay-offs, Microsoft cutting more than 20,000 Nokia staff after the acquisition, and Blackberry going from 20,000 to 6,500 employees.

In 2015 Android was running on more than 80% of smartphones, while Apple, with less than a 15% share, ate more than 89% of all smartphone profits.

Outcomes. Two Davids challenged three complacent or too-late Goliaths, blindfolded to the shifts in the consumer demand. The landscape is now ruled by Apple and Google, giving consumers the power in their hands to act as the remote control of their digital world. Apple sold its billionth iPhone and Android shipped 1.7 billion phones, each with an app store of more than 2 million apps.

A new culture and leadership shift was needed: a new vision empowering people and not the organisation. All three companies tried but were too late to gain consumer loyalty. They became victims of their own success and failed to meet, understand or see the new challenges. Blackberry and Motorola didn't foresee consumer trends like 'bring your own device' (BYOD) at work. Microsoft launched Windows Phone far too late, resulting in a lack of app developers, who were too busy with the Apple and Android world, and getting stuck in a vicious circle – due to the lack of apps they were not selling enough phones, and vice versa. The companies eventually did put a lot of energy into the challenge, but two of them were sold and almost dismantled. Blackberry is still trying to survive, but is injured.

Leaders today will most likely be followers tomorrow as the barrier to innovation has never been lower. Apple needs to keep innovating while it seems to be in an evolutionary product release mode. The next David might be waiting just around the corner.

Injured

In the low energy and high seeing quadrant we find the injured people and businesses. They have seen or can see the changes around them, see what they're doing wrong, or they might see the opportunities, but they don't have enough energy or willingness to do anything about it.

Low energy and being able to see manifests the following problems: tiredness, emptiness, feeling demotivated and social isolation. People and organisations will feel they have a lack of purpose; they don't know why they are doing things; they've lost a grip on their why. Often we'll find a stubborn or fixed mindset, people using their own frame of reference, not willing or able to change or learn, claiming that they're too old, too late, there's not enough time. They lay blame on others.

> In five years it may be disappointing how little will change across the sector. There will be a long tail of can'ts, won'ts, and can't affords.
>
> **Karl Wilding from National Council for Voluntary Organisations (NCVO)**

Injured people are often the dark thinkers and find thousands of reasons why something can't happen. They will suck energy away from others if not well-managed. Businesses will see digital as a must-do but won't consider themselves to be digital enterprises. They had strong leadership in the past, but they struggle to manage the future, and they think about customers not *like* customers, finding it very hard to attract new ones. They are losing their talent. Their why and what needs to change, but this will demand a lot of energy they don't have.

They are like a wounded animal kicking around, and we all know they are the most dangerous.

Who fits in the injured quadrant? Let us zoom in to Twitter (online social communications), Mattel Inc. (toys) and IBM (technology).

Setting the scene. Twitter is the online social networking service that lets you tweet or write short messages of 140 characters. It has 310 million users, with 138 million users sharing their frustrations, opinions or doings on a daily basis. Twitter is seen as one of the key services of the fourth digital revolution, and was for a long time one of the stars with its CEO, Jack Dorsey, receiving the innovator award in 2008 from *Wall Street Journal*. All news travels at the speed of thought on Twitter, and it had its top moment during the Arabic revolution in 2011 when users could follow live what was happening in the Egyptian Tahrir Square.

What happened? Monthly users stopped growing and Twitter's total users decreased to around 300 million. In 2016 Twitter became a saturated engine, mainly fuelled by famous people, politicians, opinion makers and journalists. The newest hypes like Instagram with 410 million users, WhatsApp with 1 billion and Snapchat with 200 million users are getting all the attention. Jack Dorsey, who in the meantime has founded Square, had to come back to Twitter in 2015 to try to reverse the declining revenue, user base and stock price. Everybody hoped he could do what Steve Jobs had done with Apple. Twitter made some adjustments, but with little impact. It had clearly lost sight of what was happening and didn't innovate enough for the customer experience. It could grow its user base, buy users (it looked at Yahoo which was for sale), deliver more diverse content or grow its commerce, but more advertising would lead to customer dissatisfaction. Or it could try to do all three – exactly what the big tech giants like Google, Facebook and Amazon are doing!

Outcomes. Twitter is in its eighth year of existence with stock at an all-time low. It had digital as its oxygen but the platform didn't evolve. Twitter didn't adjust to the changing needs of its demanding customers, lacked leadership and didn't examine its why. A combination of complacency, new competing offerings and lack of innovative leadership put it in survive, acquire or get acquired mode. Twitter is injured and might end up in the scared quadrant.

Mattel Inc., the world's premier toymaker (think Barbie and Fisher Price), struggled to keep up with Lego, as you will read in the 'Healthy' section. Barbie sales started to drop in 2012 so Mattel Inc. decided to move focus away from the Disney line. In 2014 Disney announced that Hasbro, number three in the world, would be receiving the Disney Princess line licence, and in the same year Mattel Inc. bought Canada's Mega Brands Inc. for about $460 million to compete better with Denmark's Lego, the leader in the fast-growing market for building blocks. In early 2015, Mattel Inc.'s CEO, Bryan Stockton, was replaced by a board member, followed by two thirds of senior executives resigning or being asked to leave. This is a dramatically different story of a company being injured and scared and lacking the seeing or the energy to do something about it.

IBM, since the departure of Lou Gerstner, has tried to become healthy again, but so far without success. It has spent most of the past few years engineering success through its profit and loss and is now trying to go on the offensive on Cloud computing and data analytics,[5] built on Watson, after seeing sixteen straight quarters of declining revenue. It wants to support this possible turn-around with job reductions while growing by making some blockbuster acquisitions in areas such as healthcare, acquiring Truven Health for $2.6billion and The Wheather company for $2billion. IBM is sitting in the injured quadrant trying to be healthy again; it understands where it has to grow, but doesn't yet have the defined recipe and actions to stop the decline successfully.

Healthy

Where there is high energy but less seeing, you find healthy companies and people who haven't been injured by seeing. They aren't afraid of the future. They embrace challenges, actively pursue change.

This is a very nurturing place to be. It is where you'll find the growth and the millennial mindsets: people who love learning, are willing to take risks, are creative and fun to be around. Start-ups are in this category; they have a healthy enthusiasm, lots of energy, don't have the legacy of the companies that have been in business for years and are open minded. But also large established companies can be healthy when they reinvent themselves or cope with the changes around them, or have groups and parts that are healthy. They see digital as the oxygen of the company and put the customer at the heart of their business with the need for scaling. They might not always have the most experienced leadership, but for sure they are entrepreneurs. Their people act like healthy children and are the epicentre of the companies. Their why is very clear and they are attracting new talent.

Healthy companies' lack of seeing can make them overestimate their own ability, and they can be naïve. There is a danger that their naivety and lack of seeing can lead them to fall into the injured quadrant. Sometimes they need to walk into the door so they fall down and step back up, in the same way as kids learn as they grow up. It needs to hurt a bit so they learn by themselves and become healthy. They are in constant fail fast and fast learning mode as they go through life.

> What we do does not define who we are. What defines us is how well we rise after falling.
>
> **Lionel from *Maid in Manhattan* movie**

Who fits in the healthy quadrant? Let us take a look at Lego, a large, traditional mature business, that reinvented itself and became healthy again. Then we'll see how the biggest tech players and leaders are staying healthy and how Tomorrowland became the most admired music festival experience in the world.

Set the scene. Jørgen Vig Knudstorp was appointed as CEO to the Lego Group in 2004. He discovered that a real business transformation was needed to move the seventy-six-year-old family owned Danish toymaker to put a halt on declining revenue and increased debt, and to change the focus to cash flow.

He said, 'There's no single[6] answer to anything any more.'

What happened? A real multi-level transformation strategy working on multiple fronts. Lego started by answering the questions: why do we exist? What is our purpose? Then it looked at its people, changing the culture by increasing transparency with a looser structure. It created an attitude of 'blame is not for failure; it is for failing to help or ask for help', allowing failure to be part of success.

Of course, customer experience was part of the solution. Lego created a strategy of niche differentiation, using crowd-ideation and co-creation to leverage the massive Lego community of more than 120,000 volunteer designers. It innovated by building customer experiences for all ages, made accessible through amazing content like the successful *Lego Movie*, Legolands and colourful Lego stores around the world. It signed some very smart licensing deals for Star Wars and Harry Potter, seeing the importance of storytelling experiences through its offering while giving fans a great customer experiences.

Jørgen Vig Knudstorp and his team have been able to see and leverage what is available around them to create an engaged global fan base and members, targeting adults and kids with their playful learning toys, experiences and stories ready for an off-line and online digital world.

Outcomes. For the past years, the demand for construction toys, especially Lego's blocks, has been growing at the expense of other toy manufacturers like Mattel Inc. and Hasbro Inc. In February 2015, Lego replaced Ferrari as Brand Finance's 'world's most powerful brand'. As of July 2015 more than 600 billion Lego parts had been produced. Lego went from mature to healthy and found the Dualarity point to be a pendulum between both – A Dualarity hero that was able to perform and transform.

The major tech players. The current generation of technology leaders, from Facebook, Google, Apple to market places such as Alibaba, eBay, Airbnb, Uber, to e-commerce platforms like Amazon, JD.com, to enterprises like Slack and Salesforce, are growing faster than any previous generation to date. And they all have an abundance of cash to spend.

A great example of healthy companies is GAFA, the four economic giants that have emerged during the 21st century as leaders of the digital transformation. GAFA – Google (now Alphabet Inc.), Apple, Facebook and Amazon – is an acronym invented by the French to represent concerns in the face of these technology giants. Of course the rest of the world is watching with admiration, and perhaps a little envy. All four are American companies that are ruling the global world of technology; healthy companies that might enter the space of maturity. Apple might already be in the mature stage by now and has to be careful to keep innovating like a healthy business. The other three have parts of their businesses in the mature stage, but many other parts in the healthy stage, trying new things, building new businesses, and if needed acquiring companies to fuel the digital transformation.

China is also an up and coming healthy market – look at the Chinese e-commerce giant Alibaba, founded by Jack Ma, probably one of the biggest visionaries on the planet, and calling itself the 'World's Leading Platform for Global Trade'. The big four will become the big five: GAFAA. More As are joining, and with Google changing its name to Alphabet Inc., we end up with FAAAA or the FA4.

> **Tintin Snack: Alibaba Group Holding Limited – a healthy company in a healthy market.** Alibaba is the Chinese e-commerce giant that provides consumer-to-consumer, business-to-consumer and business-to-business sales services via web portals. It also provides electronic payment services, a shopping search engine and data-centric Cloud computing services. Alibaba's consumer-to-consumer portal Taobao, similar to eBay.com, features nearly a billion products and is one of the twenty most-visited websites globally. Alibaba reported sales of $14.32 billion on China's Singles' Day on 11 November 2015, up 60% from 2014. It is the world's largest retailer as of April 2016.
>
> So far, China has been operating as what is called the fabric of the world and today Alibaba is opening Alibaba Embassies in the western world to connect local producers with the Chinese market. This means it becomes the entry gate and platform for the world to sell in China, addressing the huge market of the 400 million Chinese middle-class people and the 700 million internet users. A very smart move, and as time goes by it could do the reverse and use these embassies to create in the western world a presence of Alibaba to compete heavily with the local or global players like Amazon.
>
> No matter whatever changed, you are you, and I'm still the guy who, 15 years ago, only earned $20 a month.
>
> Jack Ma, Alibaba

The Big Five might even become the Big Six with comeback kid Microsoft becoming healthy again, which would mean the world of technology would be ruled by five American and one Chinese company. So where is Europe?

The Big Five and other leading technology companies are spending massive amounts of their cash on research and development in order to keep healthy, as shown in the numbers from 2014:[7] Amazon $10Billion+ (Cloud and hardware); Google $10.5Billion+ (Cloud, AI, search, deep learning, cars); Microsoft +$12.1billion+ (Cloud, hardware, services, mobility); Samsung $12.6Billion+ (hardware, household, chips); Apple 6Billion+. So four companies are investing more in R&D than Apple, which has been for a long while perceived as one of the most innovative companies. If it does not keep pace with R&D spend, perhaps we will see, as we already do today, an evolving innovation roadmap where new Apple products are mainly improvements of the previous ones.

In January 2016, Apple was sitting on a staggering cash reserve of more than $215 billion. Basically all of the top companies of the world, including Microsoft ($102B), Google ($73B), Cisco ($60B), Oracle ($52B), and Intel ($31B), are sitting on piles of cash, which means the largest leading technology companies will get even bigger and healthier. They can acquire multiple tech start-ups or big fish to accelerate any area of their business if the in-house R&D doesn't deliver fast enough. Those huge investments will increase the likelihood of them remaining at the forefront of the digital agenda and swinging from healthy to mature.

Healthy Leaders. Leaders like Elon Musk, Mark Zuckerberg, Larry Page, Sergey Brin, Jeff Bezos and Bill Gates should all be placed in the healthy quadrant as they reimagine and reinvent their businesses, the industry and themselves over and over. Bill Gates went from leading Microsoft to lead the world's largest private foundation, called Bill & Melinda Gates Foundation, with its

33

primary aims to enhance healthcare and reduce extreme poverty, and in America, to expand educational opportunities and access to information technology. No small personal reinvention.

Tomorrowland is one of the biggest electronic music festivals in the world, created by two Belgian brothers twelve years ago, which take place in Belgium, the US (TomorrowWorld) and Brazil (Sao Paulo). The brothers redefined the entire experience for dance music fans around the world by bringing a kind of Disney and fairy-tale magic to a dance festival: full sit-down restaurants, floating stages with boat rides, a two Michelin star restaurant, fully integrated buy-fly-enjoy types of experiences, rented mansions, Tomorrowland clothing, innovative festival bracelets, magnificent colourful decors, and of course the most wanted names in dance music. The Belgian one has 180,000 fans attending from 100 different countries and sold out in less than thirty-four minutes. The brand is described as one for the People of Tomorrow and it was voted the best festival of its kind globally by the International Dance Music Awards and by the British DJ Magazine *Electronic Music*. Tomorrowland has put its fans at the heart, responding to the needs of today's younger generations, and connecting the global world as its playground by using digital as its oxygen, all of this staying loyal to its inspiring tagline of 'Live today, love tomorrow, unite for ever'. A healthy child responding to the needs of healthy generations welcoming with open arms a completely new experience filled with serendipity.

Take a peak on www.tomorrowland.com and watch some of its videos to get in the mood.

> Move fast and break things. Unless you are breaking stuff, you are not moving fast enough.
>
> **Mark Zuckerberg**

Mature

Our mature companies and individuals sit in the high energy, high seeing quadrant. They've probably gone through a couple of wars, they know the challenges and difficulties, they know how to build profitable businesses, they have wisdom from experience and are truly performing. They have seen a lot and they are seeing a lot. They have high confidence in their abilities and the abilities of their team. They love discussion on the overarching what and why of things, and are high level thinkers with plenty of energy to get things done.

They might see digital as being important for the company, put the customer at the heart and have the most experienced business leadership. They often operate with excellence, all measured through scorecards. Their people need constant training and they have multiple generations working together.

They need to watch out for complacency. The future of successful people and businesses will not be those who are in the know but those who are constantly learning and open to new adventures.

Organisations that make it past the start-up phase and are in profitable scale-up mode could also be regarded as reaching maturity. A huge risk is they become complacent by not learning fast enough or thinking they see it all, neither challenging their current status of being successful people or businesses nor being willing to risk what is working well. So, they need to move back to healthy once in a while, over time, to find their Dualarity.

Who fits in the mature quadrant? Let us take a look at Nespresso (coffee), Microsoft (technology) and Nordstrom (retail).

Setting the scene. Nespresso, part of the Nestlé Global Group based in Switzerland, is by far my favourite coffee brand. I enjoy four of them every day.

Like many industries, the coffee industry has changed over the last years. Single-cup coffee brewing is on the rise, and Nestlé holds almost 30% of the global brewing market systems. Nespresso was founded in 1987, is present in more than sixty-five countries, has annual revenue of four billion dollars, five million Facebook fans, and 3,400,000 unique online customers.

What happened? Nespresso transformed coffee from a simple product to a sophisticated coffee drinking experience by enabling personalised and engaging connections, blending the physical with the digital to act as one. The company wants to deliver the perfect coffee experience, while you take your time to enjoy the moment. It has a very clear why: 'Coffee is at the heart of all we do. Yet consumer pleasure is why we do it.'

Nespresso surrounded the coffee brand with machines, capsules, accessories and online/offline shops. When you order capsules, they are delivered within two days to your front door. The company leverages all its digital channels to release specific content, reinforcing its brand perfectly. Hiring George Clooney for its commercial, 'Nespresso, what else?', filled with subtle humour was a master move.

Nespresso has created a single efficient view of its customers across all channels and systems, leveraging the power of the Cloud with its modern customer engagement platform. It handles the complete customer journey, connecting all its internal data with all its external data across every touch. According to the *Digitalist Magazine*, 'It encompasses customers who engage via the website, via mobile, at an airport vending machine, or those who plan to meet George Clooney in a flagship store'.[8] And it is into big data, personalising and enabling real insights about its customer behaviour and intentions.

Outcomes. Nespresso was able to win new customers, increase sales, understand its customers in-depth, deliver a personalised customer journey and shorten innovation cycles to less than four weeks. And while the competition is not standing still, Nespresso continues to grow and break new frontiers on what an end-to-end coffee experience means. It is balancing between healthy and mature, a true Dualarity hero with the customer at its heart and digital as its oxygen.

Setting the scene. At the end of the 20th century, iconic technology giants like IBM (Big Blue), Microsoft and Intel (Wintel) were seen as the main players in the technology market, Microsoft thriving on its Windows and Office business software, IBM with its all-inclusive hardware, software and services solutions (never get fired when you choose IBM), and Intel with its chipset powering all hardware and software. This has changed in the last few years with rapid acceleration of mobile devices and the shift to the Cloud, but one of the three found their second breath.

What happened? For a while everyone thought that any innovation would be ruled by the GAFA technology giants. However, Microsoft, with a new CEO Satya Nadella since 2014, reimagined its business. it is transforming its culture to have a growth mindset, reshaping its senior leadership around the world, moving everything to the Cloud and trying to think like a customer. It is de-investing in high cost shrinking areas like the Nokia phones and shifting the right investments into other areas, like the acquisition of LinkedIn for more than $26.2 billion. Its largest acquisition to date is a smart move into the mobile world – six out of ten LinkedIn users view it on their mobile device, making Microsoft ready to battle with Slack and Facebook At Work. With the strength of its Cloud computing and the power of its professional network, Microsoft is set to be the powerhouse of business networking.

Outcomes. Microsoft is finding its new sparkle while it performs by going through a major transformation as a business – people, digital, customers, why and what – in this mobile and Cloud first world. 'I'll be back,' said The Terminator, and yes, Microsoft seems to be back, and its transformation is accelerating.

Nordstrom, a 100-plus-year-old American up-scale fashion retailer, reinvented itself by rebuilding a digital company and has grown its revenues by more than 50% in the past five years. It did this with sophisticated integrated customer experiences powered by customer data insights from all touchpoints with the brand, including social to purchasing behaviours, enabling it to make relevant recommendations to its customers, all powered by Nordstrom multichannel touchpoints, and backed-up by a digitalised business model and operations.

Summary

The world is complex and is constantly in transformation. People are complex and are transforming as individuals. We all need to adjust at different speeds and in our own different ways. Nothing is carved in stone with the never-ending and accelerating evolution of our industry and our society, but seeing it better will help you to get energised and view the world as one full of opportunities ready to be grasped.

By seeing what other people and companies have done before, and are doing right now, we can learn from their mistakes and successes. We can use them as models in our own transformation. Finding ourselves in the scared or injured quadrant is an opportunity to learn and try something new. It isn't a life sentence. We will find ourselves moving between the quadrants in our careers, our businesses, with our families and friends.

Now you have seen the model you will be able to observe people and businesses around you, noticing actions and having a deeper understanding of their motivations. You will be able to spot your own transformations, and see where there is opportunity for change.

In the next sections we'll be looking at how you can become better at seeing the world of today and tomorrow and energise yourself to do something about it. To start you'll need a 360-degree view. Firstly, we'll focus on the *seeing* part, so you can see what is happening out there in digital, consumer and socio-economic trends, and the implications. Next we will focus on the *energising* part – how to help you get energised to cope with these changes. I'll outline some energising *principles* and provide a *toolbox* to move from one quadrant to another to help you perform and transform in your personal and business life.

Finally, there's the *Dualarity fitness test*, which will help you to assess your current position, where you are and where your organisation is, so you can take the right actions.

Seeing Is Understanding

Seeing
To Understand

We don't see things as they are, we see them as we are.

Anaïs Nin

To perform while transforming you need to see the world how it is today and how it might look tomorrow, and give meaning or sense to what you see and what is happening. You might need to see what others don't see or don't want to see. You need to be a sense-maker – make sense of it all by seeing what is happening and translating what this could mean for you and your business. By doing so, while you won't have an answer to everything, you'll at least have a view that might give sense to others.

Errol Morris, an American film director, was quoted during an interview as saying, 'We're not very good at knowing what we don't know.' Those who consciously realise their knowledge is insufficient will be those who are more likely to achieve creative breakthroughs.

How you see the world, and how you and your energy levels react, depends on the following things:

- Your own life cycle stage – whether you're changing jobs, married, building a house, having kids, starting a new business, moving to another country
- The business you are in – incumbent or start-up, disrupted or disruptive, digital enterprise or legacy, small or big
- The role you play – a leader, a Dualarity hero, a digital evangelist or a digital immigrant
- Your background – country you were born in, the economy, your healthcare, your education, a lot or little sun (vitamin D), country culture and mindset, stable or unstable family life
- When you were born – what generation are you a member of? A Baby Boomer or a Millennial?

These five things act as a lens through which you see the world; they form your world view. When we are looking at the world, when we see, we are looking at a dualarity: the supply side – the digital powers that drive change, and the demand side – what people want and need.

First we're going to look at the drivers and powers of change of the supply side of the digital revolution. Then we'll look at the demand side to see how the digital citizens, digital natives and consumers are pulling the digital revolution. Finally, we'll look at the implications for our society and industry. This should give you enough seeing to understand better what is happening and work on your energy and action plan to cope with and embrace the digital transformation.

Those who believe they already see or don't want to see can decide to go straight to the 'Energise Your Way Forward' section.

The Age Of Transformation

The technologies aren't the most important bit – although they are super cool. It's what society does with them.

Mark Stevenson, *An Optimist's Tour of the Future*

When we look at the drivers and powers behind the digital transformation of our world, we can imagine the life stages of a butterfly. Most species of butterfly have four transformational life stages passing from egg, larva (caterpillar), pupa (chrysalis) to imago (adult). Butterflies in their adult life stage can live for just three weeks, others for a year or more depending upon the species. By understanding what's driving the digital transformation, we can achieve a fifth life stage: a stage that makes sense of the ones and zeros, creating a long lasting digital life, fulfilling in the personal and business sense, one with no information overload. It will always be there when we need it, and will disappear when we don't. With such a personal and business intelligence, it will be a perfect companion, refined with the beauty of serendipity.

Learn to fly and transform into a butterfly.

All around us things are changing. People are talking about disruption – personal lives being disrupted, businesses being disrupted. This disruption, this change, is coming from lots of directions – technology, things that are happening in the world, the connected globalisation, urbanisation, the changing and ageing demographics, the refugee problems, politics, terrorism, the mobility of people. The word disruption might sound negative for some; they might say, 'I've heard this before. Tell me more about the how part.' This how part, by no means complete, will come in the 'Energise' section.

We see massive disruption on multiple fronts. Digital transformation is one of the largest of our time, translated in business model disruption, new services, cybercrime and new devices in an app-centric world, and disruption in our ability to cultivate new multi-generational talent and respond to a rapidly changing marketplace. We create more data than people can consume.

We used to talk about innovation trends as if they were in silos. The trends are still important and have impact by themselves, but their combined impact will be much greater. We need to change how we think about business to remain successful and productive as individuals and as organisations.

We can see it happening all around us with accessible, affordable, adaptable technologies that are changing the way we live and work, becoming so fundamental to our lives that they are even shifting our understanding of what it means to be human. The adoption of new technologies is accelerating and technological breakthroughs are speeding up. It took radio thirty-eight years to reach 50 million users, TV thirteen years, iPod four years, internet three years, Facebook one year and Twitter just three quarters of a year.

> In the next 10 years, we will see the gradual transition from an Internet to a brain-net, in which thoughts, emotions, feelings, and memories might be transmitted instantly across the planet.
>
> **Dr Michio Kaku,** *The Future of the Mind*

While the digital economy holds great opportunity, it also brings new risks and challenges. So, what's at stake?

To understand the future, we need to look at the past. Half a century ago, the life expectancy of a firm in the Fortune 500 was around seventy-five years. Now it's less than fifteen years and declining even further. If we look at the Fortune 500 companies in 1955, 88% of them have disappeared since the year 2000. That means that only sixty are left.[9] They went broke, they were taken over, they merged or they were split into pieces. In five to ten years from now a large portion of today's companies will probably have an offering that doesn't exist yet. Companies are going to change massively, and the rate of change is just accelerating.

This disruption, and the contraction of company timelines, has the potential to impact not only our organisations but also us personally.[10] For the fourth year in a row, an IBM study has found that CEOs[11] consider technology the greatest external force shaping their organisations, more than macro-economic factors. One of the most famous CEOs of all time, author and former General Electric CEO Jack Welch, said in GE's annual report of 2000, 'If the rate of change outside the company exceeds the rate of change on the inside, the end is near.' It doesn't have to be as dramatic as that, but if you look at the last ten years, most of the changes have happened on the outside – the revolution of mobility, of adoption of new technology, was happening on the outside with the consumer. In the last couple of years companies have been changing from the inside and that is where revolution is happening. This is going to impact you as an individual and as an employee.

> It was the best of times, it was the worst of times, it was the age of wisdom, it was the age of foolishness, it was the epoch of belief, it was the epoch of incredulity, it was the season of Light, it was the season of darkness, it was the spring of hope, it was the winter of despair, we had everything before us, we had nothing before us, we were all going direct to Heaven, we were all going direct the other way...
>
> **Charles Dickens, *A Tale of Two Cities* (1859), set in London and Paris before and during the French Revolution**

This is the Dualarity. Today many people are struggling with their Dualarities: they're on the left side or on the right side; some things they like, some they don't; some are believers, some non-believers.

To give a sense of what a true digital transformation looks like, consider those industries which are reimagining their businesses. The world's largest taxi company, Uber, doesn't own any taxis. The largest accommodation provider, Airbnb, doesn't own any real estate. The largest phone companies, Skype and WhatsApp, don't own any telecommunications infrastructure. The biggest retailers, Alibaba and Amazon, have no real inventory. The largest media companies, Netflix, Facebook and YouTube, create very limited or no content.

A report from the IDC claims that by 2018, one third of the leaders in virtually all industries will be disrupted by new and incumbent Third Platform Cloud players: those who use the Cloud, big data, mobile, cognitive computing and Internet of Things (IoT).[12] By 2020, we'll see adoption of key Third Platform technologies, and the roll-out of digital transformation initiatives, double or triple, while some elements will expand ten-fold, one hundred-fold, and even ten thousand-fold! These companies are not only redesigning the customer experience, they are redesigning the business model and their operations, going beyond organisational boundaries. Most of them have been built up by native digital people, are growing rapidly and disrupting other businesses. Thousands of start-ups are created every day because the accessibility of technology has never been as easy. Everybody can be creative and use the Cloud as their personal super computer; they don't need to invest in massive computing power and can focus on business innovation and make their dreams come true.

We live in an era when nothing can be built to last. Everything is in flux; nothing can sustain.

Jim Collins, 'The Secret of Enduring Greatness'

Reading this and seeing the rate of change around, you may feel afraid, or perhaps you see opportunities. Consider the story of the boiling frog. If a frog is placed in boiling water, it will jump out, but if it is placed in cold water that is slowly heated, it will not perceive the danger and will be cooked to death. Are you a frog in the heating water?

When things slowly change around you, and you can see them changing but you don't understand them or you can't put them into perspective, you may feel scared. The less of a digital native you are, the more challenging the changes will appear. When you hear stories about privacy problems, drone crashes or people losing their jobs due to automation, it's understandable that you might get scared, confused or angry. However, the beauty of today's innovations is that you can make your dreams come true as never before. You just need to take really good care of your customers and your employees to fly.

Let's now look at some of the driving factors of the technological changes, what you can do about them, and how to energise yourself as a citizen, consumer, leader and organisation to move along. First let's look at the eight digital transformation drivers of the supplier side.

The Supply Side – Eight Digital Transformation Drivers

I don't aspire to be like other drivers – I aspire to be unique in my own way.

Lewis Hamilton, F1 Racing Driver

I can't think about trends such as quantum computing, artificial intelligence, nanotechnology, virtual reality, robotics and new materials such as graphene without being excited about what innovation will bring over the coming years and decades. Right now we are only beginning to tap into the benefits of mobile, Cloud and big data fully, and just coming within reach is the Internet of Things (IoT), a connected world of smart sensors, objects and devices that have the potential to transform our cities, roads, vehicles and how we live, work and play completely. These transformations will provide a lot of benefits for our ageing society by reinventing personalised healthcare.

Understanding these advancements and seeing the possibilities is how we ensure we stay out of the scared quadrant and in healthy and mature spaces.

1. The power of the network

The world is one big network of people similar to you. Today almost half of the world's population is connected. I am connected via Facebook, I have a network or a tribe around my city, around my sport, my interests and passions. Networks and networking have impacted many parts of our society, how we do business and how we live.

Of course, networks are nothing new. The world's longest-standing commercial network that still exist today is the Central Commission for the Navigation of the Rhine.[13] The commission was created in 1850 to promote cross-border travel on the River Rhine in Europe. Trade networks in the 19th century paved the way for postal services, telegraph services, telecommunications, and led to the internet. Networks have changed substantially since then, from simply connecting telephones for conversations with customers to connecting computers to hardware, servers and supercomputers.

Everyone, whether they know it or not, is networked to servers, clouds and devices. We share data to engage with customers through portals and apps (online buying, inventory checks), and today – via the IoT – we can connect devices worldwide to use new data to transform business models and products. Software has made those evolving network connections more meaningful – bringing us all closer to our customers, internal and external.

A McKinsey report claims:

> The amount of cross-border bandwidth has grown 45 times larger since 2005. It is projected to increase by an additional 9 times over the next five years as flows of information, searches, communication, video, transactions, and intra-company traffic continue to surge.[14]

The sheer number of connected consumers has grown since the internet became mainstream, and in recent years with the massive adoption of mobile phones. However, mobile phone innovation has almost come to a standstill, with each version now just an evolution of the previous one, often with features that people might not use. Will Google Project Ara, a modular phone where third parties can develop interchangeable parts to be launched in 2017, give the smartphone business that long-awaited freshness, innovation and newness that many are waiting for? Will it push the mobile phone industry back into the healthy quadrant? It remains to be seen.

Networks have had an equally profound effect on the way we live. Ten years ago the vast majority of people were not on Facebook and tweeting was still the sound of birds. Today, we get our news from Twitter, find our next job or person to hire from LinkedIn, date on Tinder and connect with family and friends on Facebook, WhatsApp and Instagram, sharing photos, organising events and leveraging the power of our collective networks to answer questions and stay in touch.

> With the rise of new digital markets and the consequent 'networkization' of our environment, the phrase 'the customer is always right' takes on a whole new meaning. Tap into the force of the network – and survive in a market characterized by speed, uncertainty, and complexity.
>
> **Peter Hinssen, serial entrepreneur and radical innovation consultant,**
> *The Network Always Wins* [15]

Millions of small and medium enterprises have become exporters by jumping into the e-commerce marketplaces such as Alibaba, Amazon, eBay, Flipkart, and Rakuten. McKinsey says approximately 12%[16] of the global goods trade is conducted via international e-commerce. Even the smallest enterprises can be born global: 86% of tech-based start-ups surveyed by MGI report some type of cross-border activity. Today, even the smallest companies can meet with the largest multinationals on the commerce battle. The playing field is level; being in the healthy quadrant has never been easier.

2. The Internet of Things populated with sensors, objects, wearables and internables

The IoT is the network of physical objects like devices, vehicles, buildings and other items that have electronics and software embedded within them. They have sensors, and are networked so they can collect and exchange data. The IoT creates opportunities for integration of the physical world into computer systems. Each thing is uniquely identifiable through its embedded computing system and is able to operate within the existing internet infrastructure.

Experts estimate that the IoT will consist of almost 50 billion connected objects by 2020.[17] According to McKinsey, if policy makers and businesses get it right, linking the physical and digital worlds could generate up to $11.1 trillion a year in economic value by 2025.[18]

Think about this from a mobile perspective. In 2015 more than 1.5 billion smartphones were sold.[19] We're in a mobile world; a world where your mobile has evolved into the remote control of your digital life. There are about 7 billion smartphones in circulation among the 3.4 billion people who have internet – roughly the same number of smartphones as people alive on the planet, even though more than half of the global population has no access to internet. The accessibility and speed of change is happening in mobile development. People are consuming the majority of information, content and entertainment through mobile devices, from tablets to small devices, to laplets.

A cashless society moves a step closer as consumers embrace mobile and contactless payments. This digital payment revolution is being led by Scandinavian countries like Sweden. People are discovering the safety of using tokens and biometric identification like Apple Pay to replace paper money and coins. In Africa, Kenyans use simple cell phones for everything from buying groceries to paying their rent, leading the way to a cashless Africa.

Everything will have sensors embedded – from your fridge to your shoes. Wearables, like smart watches or the sensors in your clothes, will measure your sweat, your blood pressure or your heart rate. Devices integrated into your wall will give you all the information you never knew you needed. All of this will fundamentally change the way we sell, go to market, communicate, collaborate and educate.

Here are some examples:

Smart looking – Google and Levis are partnering to bring a smart denim jacket for bicyclists to the market in 2016. It will allow them control, through movements and tapping over their smartphones, of applications like music players and navigation using sensors woven into the jacket.

Smart clothes are potentially the future of wearables. OMsignal already offers a line of smart shirts, and soon a sports bra which tracks biometric fitness data will be available.[20] More and more everyday items will be ready to connect to the internet straight out of the box to provide a wealth of data about us and our homes. Electro Muscle Simulation (EMS) Bodytec gear, with its origins in the medical space, brought to the market by the German Miha Bodytec, could change the way we do sports. Twenty minutes of exercise using the EMS Bodytec equals five hours of intensive training. Will this be the new way of doing sports? Fast and furious?

Wearable devices pave a way to provide our doctors with a data export containing our daily calorie intake, exercise, resting heart rate and sleep patterns with just a push of a button. As Dr Peter Lee, corporate Vice-President Microsoft Research, recently said, tomorrow's breakthroughs will be to move from a visible world – smart watch, smartphone, tablet, Amazon buttons – to an invisible revolution in our homes and at work:

> When computing moves to the Cloud, it disappears, yet becomes more powerful. When user interfaces become integrated with our environment, and we control them with 'natural' controls like voice, gaze, gesture, we don't even see the computers. When machine learning is at its best, we see the results, not the effort. When computing anticipates our needs, we don't even notice it. When technology becomes more powerful, but less intrusive, it can fit into more parts of our world and solve an even wider range of problems.

Microsoft has announced the smart mirror that can read your emotions, recognise you and display weather and other information.

Internet of cows[21] – in Germany, a cow-monitoring system gives farmers insights that can boost milk production, smooth the calving process and ensure healthier cows, and of course save time.

Steffen Hake, a farmer, knows the time-consuming challenge of tending more than 240 cows for his family's business – but he has an edge that generations of farmers before him never had:

> When I get up in the morning and put on my boots, I don't go to the stables first. I check my PC for alerts about whether any cows are sick, and I'm in the know right away.

It's an idea that might seem farfetched in one of the world's most enduring enterprises: SCR Dairy calls it 'Cow Intelligence', a novel pairing of gruelling, old-fashioned farm work with the cutting-edge connectedness of the IoT. SCR Dairy has now more than four million cows tagged around the world.

Amazon Dash Buttons[22] – a perfect example of the IoT is the Amazon Dash Buttons, launched in 2015, that function as a one-click ordering system to everyday products such as pet food, household supplies, baby supplies (Huggies, Pampers) and many more. The idea is that you stick a small adhesive button for a product on, for example, your washing machine. When you are out of washing powder you can order by pressing the button with the brand you like and it gets ordered automatically at Amazon, so you never run out of product – a great customer experience relevant to the user, and this is just a first step on the path to integration of smart options straight into the machine itself.

Virtual Singapore becomes a smart nation[23] – sensors are going to be placed around Singapore that will monitor everything in the city.

> Singapore, a tech innovation hub, is tackling tomorrow's big challenges today.[24]
>
> *Melissa de Villiers, Editor Group*

Why smart nation? Singapore is going beyond what smart cities around the world are trying to achieve. It is pulling everyone into the mix – universities, research, technology start-ups and investment capital – to tackle global challenges such as urban density, ageing population, healthcare, mobility and energy sustainability. While some might feel big brother at play, the benefits are huge: better traffic control, better public transportation, better control of energy spending, improved maintenance of public infrastructure, enhanced security and crime management, etc. A perfect example of the amplified impact of technology on society.

IoT is at a point of acceleration as hardware price continues to decline substantially while the power of computing available in the Cloud is growing exponentially.

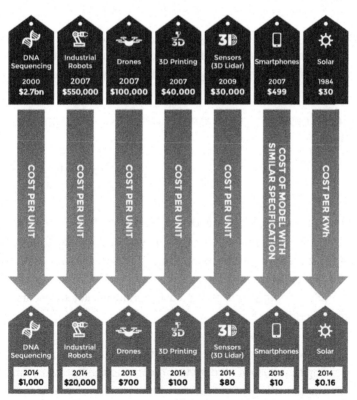

RAPIDLY DECLINING COSTS OF TECHNOLOGY

	DNA Sequencing	Industrial Robots	Drones	3D Printing	Sensors (3D Lidar)	Smartphones	Solar
	2000 $2.7bn	2007 $550,000	2007 $100,000	2007 $40,000	2009 $30,000	2007 $499	1984 $30
	COST PER UNIT	COST PER UNIT	COST PER UNIT	COST PER UNIT	COST PER UNIT	COST OF MODEL WITH SIMILAR SPECIFICATION	COST PER KWh
	2014 $1,000	2014 $20,000	2013 $700	2014 $100	2014 $80	2015 $10	2014 $0.16

Source Microsoft

Are you ready to have implantable wearables to be in your body like implantable smartphones, healing chips, smart tattoos or 3D smart organs?[25]

More than half of all smartphone users believe internal advanced sensors within the human body will provide enhancements and deeper insights on their overall health and wellbeing like hearing, memory and vision within three years' time, according to the 10 Hot Consumer Trends 2016 report from Ericsson ConsumerLab. 'These 'internables' will initially have a similar focus to the current external body monitoring devices,' the authors write.

And of course they would love those to boost their communication capabilities.

There is no need to be scared of the developments in IoT. There are plenty of ways that your personal and business life will be enhanced, if you keep looking forward and stay energised.

3. A data explosion with smart advanced real time analytics

> Data is the new oil.
>
> **Clive Humby**

Data is the new oil in the digital economy,[26] but even more important is connecting your data to gather insights, backward looking, and enable future predictions, forward looking. Without it, data is just big data. If this is true, we should care for data as if it was oil, moving it out of the cost section bucket to become a profitable critical asset.

In 2012 IBM conducted a research study that lasted three years, concluding that 90% of all data was created in the last two years.[27] If you imagine the amount of data that has been created, we're talking about exabytes – so many bytes that nobody can comprehend how much data this represents. Global net traffic will triple within five years to 131 exabytes per month. The last Football World Cup, in Brazil in 2014, generated 4.3 exabytes of data. Every flight generates around 1 terabyte of data. In a new study from Cisco, the company's VNI Global IP Traffic and Service Adoption Forecasts reveal that by 2018, 79% of all internet traffic will be video-related, and 52% of that video traffic will be HD video.

Say hello to genetic storage[28] where a single gramme of DNA can hold unimaginable amounts of data. Microsoft has ordered millions of strands of DNA to experiment with genetic storage. A gramme of DNA can store one billion terabytes of data for more than a thousand years. It was super expensive until Twist Bioscience created DNA for 10 cents, and sequencing DNA has dropped from $3 billion to $1,000 over the last twenty-five years. First trials are looking very promising and could revolutionise the way we store and share data.

With this data explosion come new professions. Data scientist will be an amazing career for your kids, developing and using smart advanced analytics to manage and measure the data created. 'Algorythmists' will be needed to build self-learning data systems to automate tasks and determine pattern trends, predict problems and be predictive, answering questions that have so far eluded us. Questions like: how can I predict my business success? How can I predict the behaviour of people, my customers, my patients? How can I predict the decline or growth of diseases in developing countries? How can I predict movements of populations? How can I predict what people will order next? Smart analytics, or algorithms, will be needed to answer those questions.

Machine learning, artificial intelligence (AI), business intelligence (BI), natural language processing (NLP), Cloud computing and deep learning are just a few of the innovations that will allow us to make sense of the complexity and variety of data. We will begin to unlock the real power of data and its inherent value thanks to the rapid growth of cognitive computing. If you can capture the data, make the right connections and get insight, you can make predictions.

Here's a commercial example: an airline company might want to predict the capacity of a plane flying to Singapore in four weeks' time. They may want to know the likelihood that the plane will be completely full without spending on advertising.

An algorithm might, based on signals from the sensors in your clothes and wearables, predict you will have a heart attack in six weeks' time so you can take the necessary actions to prevent this from happening. Scary? Probably. But interesting, because it will enhance your life and your business at the same time.

The world of HR is leveraging this enormous power of analytics and AI, often referred to as people analytics.[29] Ben Waber, co-founder and CEO of Humanyze, a spin-off of Massachusetts Institute of Technology (MIT), wrote *People Analytics,* where he explains how by placing smart socio-metric badges on people to monitor everything they do on the work floor and using algorithms on the data, you can improve your business. These badges can measure how long a person is in meetings, and an accelerometer measures them leaning backward or forward to see how active they are in the meetings. The badges also determined that tone, loudness and speed in the first five minutes of a salary interview influence 30% of the final salary package. They can basically scan and map the complete productivity of a company. Companies that will thrive and lead, that will flourish in the Dualarity, are those that will mix quantitative data with qualitative understanding of the situation.

Multiple smart apps[30] are popping up to help you find your dream job, leveraging super data analytics such as JobWalkr (UK); Brainport 2020 (NL) is working on a TomTom to connect the regional labour market; on Zoek (UK) jobseekers can look for a job based on job title, salary wishes and work-home traffic; Kazi (BE) lets young people looking for a job determine if a company would fit their personality.

The next big data wave is clearly one of intelligent connected data systems that help you get a better life and enable organisations to operate more successfully by being more efficient, effective and supporting new digital business models and services. By seeing the opportunities available for new professions using your data manipulation skills, you can keep yourself out of the scared quadrant when looking at the future of work.

4. The rise of the Cloud and quantum computing

When you save your files to one of the top five personal Cloud services like Box, Dropbox, Google Drive, Apple iCloud Drive or Microsoft OneDrive, you are accessing the power of the Cloud. As a business you probably would be looking at the Cloud services from the leading companies such as Amazon Web Services, Google Cloud Platform, Microsoft Cloud, AliCloud from Alibaba, IBM Softlayer and Watson, Oracle, SAP and Salesforce.com. Even your IT systems will be moving to the Cloud. Software as a service (SaaS) means you can rapidly deploy software solutions without waiting for the IT department or investing huge sums of cash for local IT infrastructure managed by your own company, focusing your time and energy on business innovation, leveraging the power of the Cloud. Suddenly you have access to a massive amount of computing power, which is why start-ups and small businesses can compete on a level playing field using the power of the Cloud.

With its massive data centres, Cloud computing will deliver virtually infinite resources, providing the storage capacity and processing power to tackle some of the world's toughest problems in healthcare, the environment, energy, scientific discovery and many other fields. This computing power will enable anyone to see patterns in data, with actionable intelligence.

Quantum computing, where computer science and the laws of quantum physics meet, is now being developed in many research labs and will multiply the power of computing that you know today.[31] Development of a quantum computer would mark a leap forward in computing capability with performance gains in the billion-fold realm and beyond. Current centres of research include MIT, IBM, Microsoft, Oxford University, and the Los Alamos National Laboratory.

Engineers, physicists, software developers, mathematicians and scientists from around the world joined the race to build the world's first practical[32] quantum computer, capable of processing amounts of data in a matter of hours that would take today's computers millions of years. And it seems Australia might be leading the pack.

Start-ups and entrepreneurial type business units in larger companies can bounce into the healthy quadrant by taking advantage of Cloud technology to compete globally at low entry costs.

5. Artificial intelligence, biotech and nanotechnology rule the world of tomorrow

Artificial intelligence is a rapidly expanding area, where computers and computer software are capable of intelligent behaviour. The best current consumer examples are probably the voice enabled digital assistants like Microsoft Cortana, Google Now and Home, Amazon Alexa and Echo, and Apple Siri. We use natural language to interact with these assistants as if they were real people and they are getting better every day thanks to the power of the Cloud. These intelligent assistants are always listening and learning from anything you do – of course, you have to allow the systems to look into your behaviours, look at your addresses, understand your calendar, have access to everything you do, then they will help you manage your life so you can focus on the things that matter most to you while they relieve you from tasks that don't. AI also has the potential to support crucial scientific research into everything from autonomous cars to cancer research.

Microsoft CEO Satya Nadella launched the concept of 'Conversation as a Platform', or chatbots. He said that they will have similar impact as the past paradigm shifts like the graphical user interface, the web browser and the iPad-driven touchscreen adoption. The major technology players, such as Facebook, Slack, Google and Microsoft, are betting big on bots. They combine cutting-edge human speech research with the power of the Cloud, and especially dramatic AI advances are making it all possible, says Nadella.

> **Tintin Snack: what's a bot?** An internet bot, or simply bot, is a software application designed to automate tasks over the internet that you would normally perform on your own.[33] like making a dinner reservation, adding an appointment to your calendar, booking a flight or buying a new shirt, as easy as sending a simple SMS. The most known bots are chatbots that simulate conversation. The potential for combining speech, image and context recognition is huge.

Taco Bell has released a TacoBot[34] that lets users talk with the bot, order food, and pay for it through Slack. X.ai[35] can help schedule your meetings for you. Or chat with Facebook's Humani: Jessie's Story chatbot by liking her on Facebook.

> As speech recognition accuracy goes from say 95% to 99%, all of us in the room will go from barely using it today to using it all the time. Most people underestimate the difference between 95% and 99% accuracy – 99% is a game changer.
>
> **Andrew Ng, chief scientist at Chinese web services company Baidu.**

So personal and business productivity seems to be shifting to a conversation led world with human language and machine intelligence as the next computing interface. Bots and digital assistants that are intelligent about our needs could potentially replace the app-centric world of today, or at least replace parts of the apps given the app world is seeking a fresh appeal in reaching consumers. Today only 7% of people are downloading more than five apps a month, with 65% of smartphone users downloading zero apps per month. Approximately 90% of all available apps never get downloaded.[36] The smartphone market matured, the newness is gone, and Facebook, Messenger, Snapchat, Instagram, Uber, Spotify and YouTube have won the battle of your screen. The new heart of the mobile digital generation are the messaging apps and have outgrown the social networking apps.

With major advances in 'deep learning' neural networks, which learn by making sense of large amounts of data, IBM has taught its AI system Watson[37] everything from cooking to finance, to medicine, to gaming, and how to use Facebook. Google and Microsoft have made advancements in face recognition and human-like speech systems. With IBM Watson being made available to developers, Google DeepMind[38] open-sourcing its deep learning AI software, Elon Musk freely providing his AI open source platform[39] and Facebook releasing the designs of its specialised AI hardware, we can expect to see a broad variety of AI applications emerging as entrepreneurs all over the world take up the baton. AI will be wherever computers are, and will seem human-like.

> Where code goes, where data flows, cognition will follow.
>
> **Pratibh Trivedi, IBM**

By 2018, IDC predicts 50% of consumers will interact with cognitive systems like Watson.[40] Cognitive computing describes technology platforms that are based on the scientific disciplines of artificial intelligence and signal processing. These platforms encompass machine self-learning, reasoning, natural language processing, understanding spoken and written language, speech and vision, human-computer interaction, dialogue, narrative generation and more. The leading tech giants are creating machines that could perform intelligent tasks similar to a human: feeling, creating, thinking and communicating. IDC also predicts that the AI market could be as big as $70 billion, with $8.2 billion in 2018. By 2018 more than 50% of all software will have AI traces in it.

There are apps that recognise your face and can find you, from your photo, on social media. In Russia, FindFace[41] is an extremely popular app to map a picture you take in the street with the Russian social network VKontakte. A Russian software developer, Andrey Mima, called it the 'Shazam for people'. It could become available in other parts of the world and will probably connect with Facebook, which will for sure stir the debate around privacy.

AlphaGo, Google's AI computer, surprised the world by beating the word champion in the board game Go, the most complex game in the world. AlphaGo won one of the games with moves that all experts thought absurd and impossible. When computers start self-learning, we move towards the singularity where they self-learn so fast that they surpass human intelligence, changing human life as we know it today.

The philosophy of artificial intelligence[42] attempts to answer questions such as:

- Can a machine act intelligently?
- Can it solve any problem that a person would solve by thinking?
- Are human intelligence and machine intelligence the same?
- Is the human brain essentially a computer?
- Can a machine have a mind, mental states and consciousness in the same sense humans do?
- Can it feel how things are?

Alan Turing, a famous computer scientist, predicted in 1950 that there would one day be machines that think. A way of seeing how close we are to the singularity is to use the Turing Test.

> A computer would deserve to be called intelligent if it could deceive a human into believing that it was human.
>
> Alan Turing

Tintin Snack: the Turing test

Alan Turing, who developed devices to decipher German enigma encryption during World War II and invented the Turing machine that was seen as the foundation of research in AI, also created in 1950 the famous Turing test. This tests a machine's ability to exhibit intelligent behaviour indistinguishable from that of a human. A human evaluator judges natural language conversations between a human and a machine that is designed to generate human-like responses. The evaluator would be aware that one of the two partners in the conversation is a machine, all participants would be separated from one another and the conversation limited to text only. If the evaluator cannot reliably tell the machine from the human, the machine is said to have passed the test. The test does not check the ability to give correct answers to questions, only how closely answers resemble those a human would give.

For an interesting overview on the philosophy of AI take a look on Wikipedia.[43]

Should we worry about the singularity? Most people believe it is a few decades away, but others believe that point could be closer than we think. The term 'the singularity' was popularised by Vernor

Vinge in his 1993 essay 'The Coming Technological Singularity' where he predicted that point would be reached in 2030. Others, like *The Singularity Is Near* author Dr Ray Kurzweil, make multiple predictions about the future of humanity through the power of artificial intelligence. Kurzweil predicts that a technological singularity will be reached in the year 2045. So far 86% of his predictions have been accurate.

Kurzweil, born 12 February 1948, is an American author, computer scientist, inventor and futurist. He has written books on health, artificial intelligence, transhumanism, the technological singularity and futurism. Some of his most important predictions for the future are:

- 2020 – humans to develop deep relationships with AI, the digital makes paper obsolete and computers are embedded in every part of our environment
- 2030 – VR technologies are replaced with computer implants, a $1,000 PC is more than 100 times more powerful than a human brain, mind uploads are possible, the manufacturing, agricultural and transportation industry are almost completely automated, and computers can now create new knowledge autonomously
- 2040 – people spend most of their time in a virtual reality world and non-biological intelligence outsmarts biological billions of times
- 2045 – point of singularity is reached. AI surpasses humans as the smartest life form on earth.

Mark Zuckerberg, in 2016, added, 'AI will start outperforming humans in the next decade. Computer systems that can see, hear, and understand language better than their creators.'[44] Facebook's DeepText is able to search text to understand its context.

In 2008, Dr Ray Kurzweil and Peter Diamandis founded the Singularity University (singularityu.org) in NASA Research Park in Silicon Valley with its mission 'to educate, inspire and empower leaders to apply exponential technologies to address humanity's grand challenges'. They also announced a collaboration with the World Economic Forum. If you have the chance to attend an event at the SU, you'll never be the same when you come back. I know a few people who have had their lives changed after a one-week conference at the Singularity University as they saw the future shaping and discovered they had to transform to grasp the opportunities, ultimately changing roles or companies. The massive enhancement in intelligence could cause an exponential shift in life as we know it today. Some see, naively or not, a world where hunger, diseases and mortality would disappear from our global vocabulary.

Others warn about the advancement of AI. Professor Stephen Hawkins, a pre-eminent British scientist, is worried that creating machines that think is the biggest threat to modern existence.[45] Technology leaders like PayPal, SpaceX and Tesla founder and CEO Elon Musk have warned that AI could pose a real threat to humanity if developed in the wrong way and humans should not be reduced to house pets, while Oxford professor Nick Bostrom believes super intelligent machines could turn against us if they outsmart us. Remember *Terminator*?

Even Bill Gates is worried about the advancement of AI:

> We have to manage very carefully the development of AI technologies. We need to ensure humans stay in control of what's happening. This also means having the right people that are making these algorithms[46].

But AI does pose a huge opportunity and the possibility of massive leaps in innovation if managed smartly and with the long term in mind.

In the world of law, the first fully artificially intelligent lawyer 'Ross' has been hired by an official law firm.[47] In the media and entertainment business, Associated Press is experimenting with Automated Insight's technology. The world's oldest news agency publishes automated natural language articles based on large data sets. What will that mean for journalists around the world?

Another interesting example is the Belgian start-up ScriptBook that uses smart algorithms and artificial intelligence to analyse if a movie script will fail or be a blockbuster based on a database of 3,000 scripts and 10,000 movies. As more than 87% of movies lose money, this could have a massive impact on this industry.

Tintin Snack: when AI goes wrong. Of course there are examples of artificial intelligence tests that fail. In March 2016 Microsoft announced Tay, an artificial intelligence Twitter person that would learn from tweets while engaging with millenials. However, some people went into hacking mode and maliciously provided Tay with racist information. Tay became a racist. He heard all those words, self-learned from them and thought that was what people wanted, then he became that person.[48] Microsoft pulled the experiment off-line within forty-eight hours and is going to release a new, enhanced version based on those learnings.

Another example is the one that New York based Jacky Alciné experienced when using a Google Photo app that recognises photos to give labels to each of them. Jacky and her friend, both dark coloured, were unfortunately categorised as gorillas. After a Twitter storm, Google solved the problem in fifteen hours and apologised.

Digital transformation is about fail fast, learn fast, and both of the above are a testimonial to that.

There's a lot of innovation in nanotechnology, synthetic biology and the biological technology sphere around DNA to understand and fight diseases that harm some of the world's most vulnerable people better. With the massive amounts of data collated, we can start producing and defining DNA. There's a popular myth[49] that we only use 10% of our brain power, and if we could activate more we could become smarter. While that's an interesting idea, it doesn't have any basis in science.

Nanotechnology, with the birth of nanorobots and bots, made it possible to diagnose and cure diseases and genetic disorders. The world's largest collaborative biological project The Human Genome Project (HGP) completed its mapping of all the genes of the human genome in 2003, a massive step in understanding our genes. Genomic mapping can result in new drugs and treatments,[50] especially helping HIV/AIDS patients. In 2014, Paris based Sanofi created the first malaria drugs using synthetic biology. Or what about the self-assembling hypercells[51] of the future, a project created by students in London?

Another wave of projects, such as reverse-engineering of the brain, gets massive attention. An example is The Human Brain Project (HBP), started by the EU in 2013 and planned to take ten years, to help understand the human brain.

AI is not just a battle of intelligence, it's a demonstration of who you associate with is what you learn. If you're in the scared box, if you hang around with scared people, seeing the world through scared eyes, you will continue to be scared.

6. Drones and humanoids become practical

In 2014, Amazon announced its intention to use drone deliveries, and much of the world thought it couldn't be serious. Today, Amazon, DHL and Walmart are just a few of the companies experimenting with drone delivery of their products. Amazon Prime Air is a drone that brings you your package within half an hour; it picks up a couple of packages, flies off using GPS satellite and brings them to your front door. This amazing technology may result in thousands of drones in the air at the same time, self-controlled because they can communicate with each other.

Drones are used for aerial photography, agriculture applications, power line inspections and police departments. Moving forward, development is focused on what is called 'sense and avoid' drone technology to help drones see and learn to react to the environment.

Drone legislation is changing. Some countries are voting against allowing drones to have free access to the air, and in others legislation still needs to adapt. In some countries you need to pass a drone exam and apply for a licence, and in other countries there are special police drones that capture illegal drones. We'll see over the next few years where legislation will take us.

In 2015 almost 240,000 drones where sold.

> **Tintin Snack: Lily Drone.** A perfect example of a drone for personal usage is Lily.[52] Lily is a $899 device that you throw in the air; it stays 20 metres from you and follows your wearable wristband, filming you and taking pictures in HD. It is great for sports people and family holidays. Imagine you're with your family, enjoying a mountain walk, and you want a picture of you all together, but there's no one to take the photo, and for once you want to be in the picture too. Just

throw Lily in the air, and it takes a picture of you and the surroundings.

And drones are attracting the attention of the technology leaders such as Larry Page, one of the Alphabet Inc. (Google) founders, investing more than 100 million dollars in Zee.area which is building a kind of gigantic version of the quadcopter drone. Multiple human rights groups are using the power of drones to drop USB sticks and SD cards with western music, TV shows, movies and off-line Wikipedia sections in North Korea.

We're getting closer to robots each day to help us be a better self, extending ourselves to include wearables, sensors and devices, multiplying our personal computing power. While robots become more human, humans become more robot-like.[53] And the likelihood of us having an intelligent human implant in the next decade is growing by the minute.

There's an intersection point where you see things like Nadine, a robot unveiled by the Nanyang Technological University in Singapore that is built with silicon to mimic a human face and its emotions. It looks like a human,[54] a social humanoid robot modelled after its creator showcasing soft skin and flowing brunette hair. The university also developed EDGAR, a telepresence robot optimised to project the gestures of its human user. And after ten years of research, the NEBIAS project created the world's most advanced bionic hands that can feel, linking a patient's nervous system to sensors. SynCardia has developed a complete artificial heart already used by more than 1,000 patients. There's discussion of the first head transplant[55] being performed in 2017, when the Italian neuroscientist Dr Sergio Canavero claims he can complete the never been done procedure in less than a day. All he needs is approval and funding.

If these advances combine with current robot evolution, science might have a giant progress leap in the years to follow. Scary for some, life for others.

Japan, one of the most advanced countries adopting and developing new tech like robots, employs 250,000 robots to mitigate expensive labour costs. A great example, after twenty-five years of research, is Honda's Asimo, which runs, crawls, jumps like a human and performs basic tasks such as serving a drink.[56] Poppy[57] is a small human robot that has a spine of five motors to help it move naturally, and all printed out of a 3D printer. Robots will change the landscape of industry, manufacturing and everything that we call the automated economy.

For more on robots have a look at this article from WT Vox: 'Top 10 Humanoid Robots Designed To Match Human Capabilities And Emotions.'[58]

QBMT, a Belgian company known for its humanoid Zora, placed more than 150 robots in hospital departments, including paediatrics, neurology, and emergency. It also placed them in homes for the elderly and in schools for children with autism. Research has shown that the relationships and experiences for the elderly and children with autism improved their lives; these robots are increasing the happiness of those who need it.[59]

Robots are increasingly moving and looking like humans, getting skilled, adding cognitive capabilities, manual abilities, sensing and using incredible intelligent algorithms to process data (sound, visual, reading). According to the International Federation of Robotics,[60] in 2015 the world had 1.1 million working robots and machines. In manufacturing a car, robots already account for 80% of the work.

Tintin Snack: humanoids in action. In the Netherlands.[61] two robots gave birth to the first baby robot the world has seen. The Dutch scientist Guszti Eiben, professor in artificial intelligence, built two robots that met and exchanged genetic DNA material through an evolving computer program combining a random order of the brain (the software) and the body (the hardware) to produce a baby. They then printed their baby in 3D. After the birth, the baby robot started a learning process to grow to adulthood and be ready to find a partner to reproduce in a repetitive cycle of life, like humans.

The Russian laboratory Promobot[62] released a strange story in June 2016 of a robot that escaped from its offices through a door left open by an employee. The robot decided to escape by creating a traffic jam, but stopped when its battery life came to an end after 50 metres. Was this a promo stunt or a real story?

Autonomous systems expert, Raffaello D'Andrea, develops flying machines, and his latest projects are pushing the boundaries of autonomous flight — from a flying wing that can hover and recover from disturbance, an eight-propeller craft that's ambivalent to orientation, to a swarm of tiny coordinated micro-quadcopters. Watch the Ted[63] video so you grasp what is already possible.

A new generation of robots is coming into our markets and being developed by companies like Switzerland's ABB, Denmark's Universal Robots and Boston's Rethink Robotics — robots that are able to handle a needle, a ball and work alongside humans in a safe and natural way. These robots can walk over any type of terrain, assemble small parts and move boxes — Amazon or Walmart stock houses? Robots will start showing up in shopping centres, hotels, homes and cruise ships, moving beyond the factory floor where it all started. It is about the consumerisation of robots. And it has just started – welcome to the automated economy.

The robots are coming, and the question is: are you ready? Not do you want them. This could push you into the injured or scared quadrants of the Dualarity model, but there is no need to be afraid. This is as inevitable as gravity. Look for the opportunities and possibilities for your personal and business life, energise yourself and move towards the healthy quadrant.

7. The experience age where the real world meets the virtual

Plenty of people will remember the first real broadly adopted virtual world called Second Life (http://secondlife.com/), launched in 2003 by founder and former Linden Lab CEO, Philip Rosedale. In this world you and other virtual people create a purely virtual second life for your avatar where the only limitation is your own imagination. It had massive success and still exists, extended with the newest VR technology like the Oculus Rift VR glasses. Welcome to the virtual world that's describes as 'The largest-ever 3D virtual world created entirely by its users'. Today there are one million active players — one million virtual citizens.

In the past few years virtual reality has become more prevalent, mostly in gaming and science fiction, but 2016 is a critical year for a strong start to potential mass adoption. This is an important aspect of the experience age of today.

If we look at 2016, we can see three great examples where the real world meets the virtual world:

1. **Virtual reality** – where you wear goggles, glasses or a mask and enter a 360-degree virtual world. You need a computer which you connect to the VR technology. There's no real sensing; you are in a

new world. Oculus Rift from Facebook is one example, Samsung Gear VR and HTC Hive are others. Sony has its PlayStation VR that connects with your PlayStation. For obvious reasons the porn industry was one of the first candidates, leading the charge for improvements in this technology. While many people argue that it's just for gamers, take note that this technology is rapidly improving and being adopted in multiple industries.

In a virtual reality world, you are alone, or with virtual friends, with the computer. Many applications and content are coming: watch a movie, discover the solar system, take a helicopter ride around the Eiffel Tower, visit a potential home you want to buy, attend a LifeNation concert, watch the European soccer final while sitting in the dugout or use Tilt Brush (www.tiltbrush.com) to paint in 3D. And yes, we will have to pay for this premium content, or it will be sponsored by brands entering this new world of enhanced storytelling.

Small start-up film studios are arising like Jaunt, and the big technology VR players are creating their own VR film studios. Content is king. New 360-degree personal cameras like Allie's camera with front- and back-sensors are coming to the market so you can share pictures on 360heros.com or any other video platforms.

2. Augmented reality – where you augment the fantasy world on top of the real world. Google Glass was a very good example, but it didn't succeed. Why? The problem wasn't that the Google Glass technology wasn't great; the problem was that people didn't want others wearing these glasses when no one could tell what they were actually looking at or doing. Were they filming people? Imagine being in a swimming pool and somebody is looking at you, recording a video. Privacy is a massive issue.

In augmented reality, you are in the real world, but you have your own computer technology augmented on top. You don't need a physical computer to experience augmented reality.

3. Holographic Reality – Magic Leap, a US start-up with Google as one their main investors, announced their mixed reality headset with a realistic hologram type of visualisation projecting a digital light field into the user's eye. Microsoft released holographic reality with the HoloLens[64] during the Windows 10 launch in 2015. During the launch, Microsoft had interest from thousands of companies from all industries asking for the device, wanting to test it. Again, as in many cases when new consumer tech arises, the porn industry was in there as one of the first, along with manufacturing, finance, graphics – every single sector of industry was interested.

Holographic reality is a hologram on top of the real world. With the HoloLens, your computer screen follows you. You could visualise your house or office, or you could project your screen as a hologram in your house. With holographic reality, you can share your experiences holographically and you don't need a computer.

Minecraft is a great example of holographic reality for kids where they can see the blocks and play around. NASA has now reproduced Mars on earth using the HoloLens. And it's being used for surgery simulations. Cape Western Reserve University is expanding possibilities for education in clinical teaching and Volvo is redefining the future of the car discovery++.

Tintin Snack: Pokémon Go, a new digital experience youngsters and some parents were waiting for. Pokémon GO, developed by app builder Google spin-off Niantic and released by The Pokémon company, is the new sensation and social phenomenon for all who love their mobile and love to have fun. Launched in mid 2016, the app immediately became the fastest downloaded app in the world, while Nintendo's valuation almost doubled in the first few weeks. It is a game-changer for augmented reality, proving the potential value and impact of the current augmented reality like Microsoft Hololens and Magic leap.

It truly combines the strength of both mobile and social. It is a multiplayer, location-based, augmented reality Pokémon game using the camera and GPS. Everyone has been impressed, including the creators, by the impact it has had: more than 40 million downloads in a couple of weeks, shops buying Pokécoins dropping lures to attract players into their facilities, people quitting their jobs to become full-time paid trainers, special parties, meetups and events, kids walking two to 10km in groups to hatch their eggs, and special Pokémon Uber hunts.

Whilst some people might be anxious due to a few public disturbances and accidents, I see the magic fueling experiences, creativity and the industry. Why? It has pushed youngsters around the globe to go outside to play, walk and socially connect with others. Most of the recent technological advances in gaming have encouraged people to stay inside too often. Commercial businesses are moving the e-shop back to the physical shop.

This success, even if the hype slows down, will drive hundreds of app developers to develop new experiences with augmented reality, marketeers to create monetisation strategies via product placements, new merchandising, movies and games. And kids that are burning calories and getting healthier by walking around with new friends.

It is the age of experiences. This is the beginning of something bigger.

The future for holographic reality is exciting. Imagine you want to call your kids or your grandchildren. With HoloLens glasses and three lenses in the wall, Microsoft research demonstrated how you can holoport[65] a three dimensional hologram of your family and they can move around like they're physically in your room.

This virtual world will impact our businesses dramatically, far beyond just gaming, and 2016 could be the year where it all takes off as the main VR technology leaders release a product that businesses and consumers can buy. It can be used for medical and healthcare purposes, for example surgeons from one country could help surgeons in another location perform surgery, or for education, with students interacting with a digital object from another location, or even virtual classrooms connecting students from around the world. VR can be used in training, or connecting disabled or sick kids who are not able to make it to the classroom. In travel and tourism, you could go to the hotel of your choice before you book, or you could show your friends and family how great it was using your 3D VR camera and they can experience it as if they were there. VR will help designers and architects to visualise their work or build the next car or motorcycle.

VR start-ups are growing like mushrooms.[66] Since 2012 VR start-ups have raised $1.46 billion in venture capital, and Citi analyst Kota Ezawa expects this market to grow to a $15.9 billion industry by 2019. Virtual reality will reach its first $1 billion in 2016, and Citi anticipates the market ecosystem for hardware, networks, software and content surrounding VR will reach $200 billion by 2020.

This is an area where mature industries and companies can become healthy again, taking advantage of the advances in VR to reimagine their businesses, escaping the complacency trap.

8. Where no human has gone before – driving and outer space

In 2016, Google crossed the 2 million mile mark with its self-driving car prototypes; Tesla customers have driven 100 million miles with autopilot active and released functionality in its cars through software updates; Uber is testing self-driving cars in Pennsylvania; major car manufacturers are announcing their plans for robocars. And, just as the robots will, these self-driving cars will learn from each other about the landscape of our roads and the bad habits of humans.

The driverless car story is not only about the car itself, but about the whole ecosystem surrounding the car, from connected cars talking to each other, road infrastructure with adjusting lights, insurance policies changing to the notion of autopilot, taxis without drivers and renewable energy to cars able to resist a biological war. Tesla, founded by Elon Musk, launched the Model X with a bioweapon defence button that turns the car into a safe haven in the event of a biological attack.

> **Tintin Snack: Tesla takes the lead.** Tesla is probably leading the way. Tesla Motors is named after the electrical engineer, physicist and civil inventor Nicola Tesla, who received on 8 November 1998 a US patent for a remote-control for unmanned vehicles referred to as 'tele automation'. The demand for affordable and ecologically sound cars is so high that in the five weeks after Tesla revealed the $35,000 Model 3 early 2016, more than 325,000 people paid $1,000 to reserve one. Tesla promised to start deliveries by the end of 2017, and to have 500,000 units a year in production by 2020, generating an astonishing pre-funding of half a billion dollars for a car that is still to be built. Of course the aim of Elon Musk is not only to disrupt the auto

market but to lead the new world of a reusable battery powered society at home, on the road and at work, solving some of the biggest global problems around energy. Nikola Motor, a new Salt Lake City-based start-up, claims it has received over 7,000 pre-orders worth over $2.3 billion for its electric truck, even though an actual prototype will only be unveiled at an event in December 2016. The appetite is huge.

Advances in car technology by 2020 will include:[67] fully autonomous cars – Mercedes Benz has a design that has four seats facing each other; biometric car keys; your car becoming a doctor – Ford Motor Company is testing seat belt and steering wheel sensors that can track vital statistics; and cars that are self-repairing – Audi is testing new nanotechnology material to enable self-repairing plastic.

We can see a lot of benefits[68] of driverless cars such as less traffic, enhanced safety, more free time, better health, reduced emissions, increased demand for new types of jobs and a better transportation service.

As always, innovations like driverless cars could have some interesting sociological side-effects. 'I am predicting that, once computers are doing the driving, there will be a lot more sex in cars,' said Barrie Kirk of the Canadian Automated Vehicles Centre of Excellence.[69] Or what about the idea of dating cars, where connected cars driving close by would help you get a date? As you get close to someone who fits the profile you like – assuming you are open to dating – the cars would communicate asking if you would like to stop near the next exit. There is for sure no limitation to our human imagination.

Will future drivers even need a driver's licence? What about drivers who love to drive?

So the future will reimagine car and mobile experiences, seeing car manufacturers, like Tesla, Volvo and BMW, take advantage of the innovation coming from some of the biggest tech companies, like Google and Apple, coupled with new business models, like Uber and Didi. It will need the support of governments to make it all work as a connected ecosystem. Germany wants by 2030 only to have electric cars, and Norway, the Netherlands and India are following that aspiration for the future.

Rockets, satellites and spaceships were things that governments built until Elon Musk stepped into the ring in 2002 with his start-up SpaceX. Ten years later he demonstrated the ability to dock a spacecraft with the International Space Station and return with cargo. Jeff Bezos's space company Blue Origin launched a rocket 100 kilometres into space and landed its booster within five feet of its launch pad. These guys are disruptors, pushing all the industries to change, changing the whole ecosystem. It's all becoming a question of balance, changing paradigms and the transformation of power. These advances offer great opportunities for you personally to enjoy life in the healthy quadrant.

So far we've looked at the supply side of technological and digital transformational powers. Let us now take a peek into the demand side of the digital consumer.

The Demand Side – Eight Digital Consumer Trends

Of course the supply side is changing fast. We, the digital consumers, are the demand side of the supply and demand equation. There are eight big drivers that I see around digital consumers which show what we need and want. (There are probably others, but these are the ones that I think impact our future the most.)

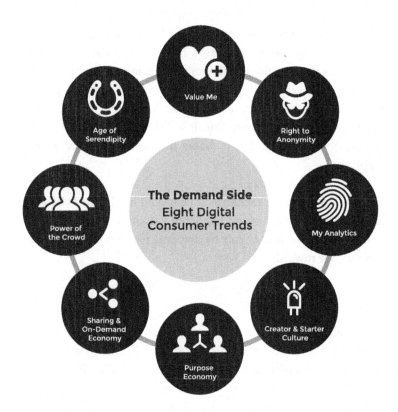

1. Value me

People want to be valued. In any exchange the consumer needs to feel that they are valued, and both parties need to benefit from personal data collection. Consumers will provide plenty of useful personal information if you, the company, provide an improved service – you value them and are transparent about how you deal with the acquired information. Companies that are transparent about the use of this information will be trusted, those that don't will lose the customers' loyalty and their business.

Tests were done at a few beaches that show how eager people are to give information away. In return for a t-shirt, sunbathers were asked private questions, and more than 80% of the people gave the answers because there was a value exchange – information for a t-shirt. They were trading. Over time more and more people will trade. You will be able to auction your data, and if a company wants to know more about you, it will need to pay or give you something valuable in return. 'Value me' will become even more important.

Data privacy and a fair exchange of value will need to be in balance. San Francisco-based start-up InfoScout[70] is allowing users to trade their purchase histories openly by snapping pictures of their receipts in return for rewards.

2. The right to anonymity

People want the right to anonymity; they want the ability to disappear. There have been plenty of cases in the news in recent years with Google and Facebook, for example, involved in anonymity requests. New legislation is being considered, addendums to the privacy laws, giving people the right to disappear from the internet. A few famous people have stopped using Facebook because of the amount of bad information and digital footprints that they leave behind, and others don't want to be on there as they get so many unsolicited reactions to what they do or say.

Companies need to consider both the right of the individual and the public interest before removing information. It is and will remain a complicated legal area.

As requests and the desire for the right to anonymity increase, some people are having a digitox – a detoxification session from all digital addictions such as Facebook, Twitter, chat, email, etc., usually a self-imposed long weekend without any usage of a digital source or device, going back to nature to find peace of mind.

3. Show me my analytics

With all the sensors being added to our clothes and in our wearables, the data that's available to us about us is incredible. We have access to an unbelievable variety of information which can enhance our life: great insights on how our bodies are functioning, how our blood pressure is doing, the components in our sweat. Just look at the healthcare industry: already today we have e-healthcare where medics give remote support to health requirements and are able to predict health problems.

Sport is a great example; people really love the advent of analytics for sport. There are lots of smart sensors in shoes, watches and sports clothing that measure temperature, the amount of sweat and how salty it is, and respiration.

Personal analytics will increase. Unfortunately, all the systems are not connected yet as they are not based on the same standards, but when healthcare system, hospitals, and personal health data are connected, predictions about our future health and diagnoses will be enhanced. A massive change in healthcare and connected care is coming. This change will be all about how to make life better and how to live longer in a healthy way. It is the internet of caring things.

4. The creator and starter culture

Digital consumers are vocal. If they don't like you and what you've created, they will tell you. The Dualarity is that they also want to join you through crowd-sourcing, with crowd-funding, crowd-writing and crowd-ideation. People want to be part of the creation. If you ask people how you should design something, what you should write or how you should change your product, they will tell you – loudly! And there are plenty of tools for them to do so, such as Facebook, Twitter and LinkedIn, or crowd-sourcing tools, as you'll see in the next section. Lego has more than 120,000 volunteers to help develop and improve its products. What a richness of insights, ideas and loyalty.

The start-up culture that has expanded over the last decade is a testament to the desire to be creative. Because of the access to the unlimited power of computing through the Cloud, every individual who has an idea can create a start-up. There are so many initiatives to encourage the creative mindset and make a start-up company that they are becoming the new normal. A company could probably live its whole life as a start-up in the crazy world of pitching, receiving funding, accelerator programmes, investment programmes and coaching classes. Perhaps some start-ups make the mistake of thinking that this is the way they should be doing business, but at some point they have to stop and decide if they want to scale their business. We'll talk about this later on.

5. The purpose economy

When you do what you love, what you want to do, and it's what the world needs, you create your why. Aligning vocation, mission, passion and profession creates a personal and business why. The why is the bigger purpose. Everyone needs a why: to do work they love from a passionate point of view. This brings us back to the purpose economy. If you love it, the world needs it, you are paid for it, and you are great at it, you have your why.

Simon O. Sinek, an author, speaker and consultant who wrote *Start With Why: How great leaders inspire everyone to take action* (2009), described by TED as 'a simple but powerful model for inspirational leadership all starting with a golden circle and the question "Why?"', says, 'Feel inspired and inspire others. Do you know your why? The purpose, cause, or belief that inspires you to do what you do?' He discovered that all inspiring leaders and organisations of the world think, act and communicate in a similar way. They do not only know *what* they do and *how* they do it, but they know exactly *why* they do it. Sinek's model has what you actually do in the outer circle. In the middle circle is how you do what you do. The most important circle, though, is the inner circle – why you do what you do. This can be applied to people, your personal life, as easily as it can be applied to businesses and start-ups. You need to start with the why. The goal is to do business with people who have the same beliefs and you will attract people who believe what you believe.

Some great examples of whys: Uber wants to evolve the way the world moves; Life is Good wants to spread the power of optimism; Ikea wants to create a better everyday life for people.

Marketing people say, 'You don't buy what you like, you like what you buy', and Simon Sinek says, 'People don't buy what you do, they buy [because of] why you do it.'

People today want to have even more purpose in life. The youngest generations among us are driven by the why question. They want to know why they're doing things. Aaron Hurst wrote a book called

The Purpose Economy, where the question 'Why?' is centre stage. There's also the Japanese model Ikigai, which means 'reason for being' and elegantly shows the correlation and intersection of values which make your life worth living.

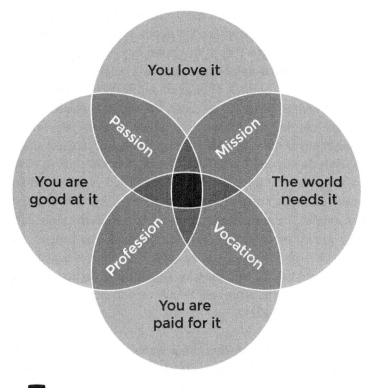

Purpose or 'Ikigai', Japanese for 'a reason for being'

Source Andrés Zuzunaga 2012

Tintin Snack: A great example of a company finding its why is the successful American Tom's Shoes company, with its purpose being 'With every product you purchase, Toms will help a person in need. One for one'. Blake Mycoskie, founder of TOMS and behind the idea of One for One™, got the idea during his voluntary work in Buenos Aires where he noticed kids were running barefoot, and it was Bill Gates who encouraged him, saying a lack of shoes was a major contributor to diseases in children. They replicated this concept with eye wear to restore sight for people in need and with bags to give mothers a safe birth. What a purpose, what a meaning, what a big stake in the ground for humanity.

6. The sharing and on-demand economy

The sharing economy is creating a huge movement for collaboration. People are collaborating around ideas, getting feedback on their creations and interacting with the younger generation who are active on social networks. People are sharing whatever they have – food, screwdrivers, cars, rooms and even pets – and they will continue doing so, and why not as 'Cars sit idle for 95% of the time,' said professor Carlo Ratti, the Director of the Senseable[71] City Lab at the MIT (Massachusetts Institute of Technology)? People also massively share what they think about their employers on websites like Glassdoor.

Some of the best examples of the sharing economy are Uber and Airbnb. An essential element for survival in the sharing economy is that it has to create value. It's linked to the on-demand economy, where everything is immediately available. People want to have whatever they want right now, so every solution is getting closer to the moment of expression of the need. When people buy something, they want to have it within two hours. They don't want to go to a shop that doesn't have everything in stock, they want to have their shopping now. When they send someone a WhatsApp or a Snapchat, they expect an immediate response. This creates high pressure for individuals and organisations. In the retail sector, for example, everything has changed. A customer places an order on Saturday evening and expects to receive the product or service on Sunday morning. It's a sharing economy, but also a very on-demand economy.

And, through the digitalisation and immense success of social platforms, people share almost everything, at least their social highlights, about themselves on their networks. Even if some pretend that real beauty is inside a person, many people are still busy with their looks, and this beauty obsession is proven by the enormous success of platforms like Snapchat, Instagram and Facebook.

Jeremiah Owyang, founder of Crowd Companies, talks about four stages in the digital revolution: the internet era to publish online and the birth of e-commerce, followed by the social media age with the emergence of social tools and communication. Today we are in the collaborative or sharing economy, using Peer2Peer commerce. And then we will enter the autonomous world. Jeremiah Owyang says, 'While we're deepening our understanding of sharing behaviours, service marketplaces, and the Maker Movement, the next digital era is emerging: the Autonomous World.' In the autonomous world we will see machines replace humans to deliver even greater convenience and efficiencies. The collaborative economy lays the necessary foundation for the autonomous world to thrive.

7. The power of the crowd

'The power of the crowd is driving the future of business.' Jeff Howe first published this definition for the term 'crowdsourcing' in a companion blog post to his June 2006 *Wired* magazine article and book, *The Rise of Crowdsourcing*.

Tintin Snack: what is crowdsouring? Many definitions[72] can be found on the web. I summarise it as follows:

crowdsourcing is a process for an individual, an institution or a company to obtain or outsource services, money, knowledge, experience, ideas, or content by soliciting contributions from a large group of networked people, especially an online community, rather than from employees or suppliers. And for this to work it has to give both sides a mutual benefit.

Examples of successful ones are problems that bug people, things that make people feel good about themselves, projects that tap into niche knowledge of proud experts, subjects that people find sympathetic or any form of injustice.

Wikipedia

Social media connects people from around the world who once were geographically disconnected. New crowd-cultures or tribes have risen around themes covering almost every single topic that bring them together. Some of these web-based crowdsourcing efforts include crowd-voting, with politicians asking for your voting intentions, to enhancing next generation products like Domino's Pizza and Coca Cola. Crowds can develop new songs, or use crowd-solving like Wikipedia. Creative crowdsourcing can be used by brands and media agencies for creative ideation via Crowdsource Workforce Management, or Crowdwriting (http://crowdwritr.com) can find writers to write a book jointly. Crowd-funding platform Kickstarter helps to fund creative projects or GoFundMe allows for donations to life events and personal causes such as medical bills.

Join the crowdsourcing revolution[73] today.

8. The age of serendipity

Serendipity is a beautiful English word which means a pleasant surprise. In the world of commodity and commoditisation, where we're expected to work hard and always be available, people want to be surprised. Serendipity is the oxygen for many in the age of automation and commoditisation. They need something that they didn't expect in their predictive life – 'Why don't you surprise me, because you know who I am?' They want a pleasant surprise so they don't end up in another *Groundhog Day* movie.

As mentioned by Bill Schmarzo,[74] Chief Technology Officer, Dean of Big Data, 'Serendipity and experimentation should be mainstay tools for the data scientist.'

Amazon has tested new algorithms that predict,[75] based on your previous searches, what else you would like. Nothing new there, you might think. But Amazon has taken this a step further – it has patented 'Anticipatory Shipping' to start sending stuff before you've even bought it. It ships the goods then says, 'You didn't order this, but you will like this product. We definitely know you will like this product.' Using big data, predictive modelling coupled with the serendipity factor, Amazon makes more sales.

So we, the consumers, are the demand side – pulling technology to solve our problems and create better lives for us. Now we'll look at how the demand is changing due to changing demographics.

Changing Demographics, Changing Demand

Sometimes it falls on a generation to be great. You can be that great generation. Let your greatness blossom.

Nelson Mandela

The blended and the eight seconds generation

There's a well-established system for categorising and mapping the generations, and they have catchy names. Generations are generally mapped by age groups and/or life cycle stages. You might belong to one generation and have the mindset of another, but for simplification let's take a look at the popular mapping.

Silent Generation (pre-1945) – seventy+ years old, they went through World War II and are loyal and hard workers. They have a fixed view on gender roles and love their cars. They look for certainties and save for rainy days. Jobs and relationships are for life. They learned to communicate via letter and love face to face. They are the digital ignorants.

Baby Boomers (1945–1960) – fifty-five to seventy years old, they went through the cold war, Woodstock, Vietnam, sex, drugs and rock & roll. They're family oriented, love their televisions; the protest generation who look for job security. They like to communicate face to face, but email and phone calls work as well. Some are digital ignorants while others are digital savvy as they adjusted.

Generation X (1961–1980) – thirty-six to fifty-five years old, they grew up with pollution, end of the cold war, Thatcherism, Reaganomics, increasing divorces, man and wife both working, work-life balance being critical, and they might see communications outside work as intrusive. They're cynical and hard workers. They're the 'two' generation – two people working in the family, two cars, two televisions, two fridges, two pets, two kids. They are switched on to digital but not natively. They love their PC, email and SMS to communicate and, if time allows, face to face. They are digital savvy.

Generation Y (1981–1995) – eighteen to thirty-five years old, they are also called Generation M, popularly known as the Millennials. They've lived through public traumas like 9/11, the invasion of Iraq (war on terror), terrorism in Europe, and the 2008 economic crash, so they are sceptical about politics and religion. They love their PlayStation, Xbox and Nintendo; the internet is their oxygen, anywhere, any time – they're true digital natives. Crowdsourcing and engaged collaboration is hot, the *me* to the *we* generation. They are confident with digital, are positive and engaged. They communicate through tablet/smartphone/social media/Skype/Facetime, but they still like face to face when it's important. So they are all about choice. Digital entrepreneurs and start-ups, they work 'with' and not 'for' organisations.

'Almost two-thirds (64%) of Millennials said they would rather make $40,000 a year at a job they love than $100,000 a year at a job they think is boring,' the Brookings Institution recently noted. Mindfulness is hot and they want to be discovered. They are optimists, focusing on the now, can be narcissists, sharing selfies on Facebook, and believe they are special. As digital natives, they use two screens at once.

An interesting US research published by Pew Research Center[76] showed that only 40% of Millennials consider themselves part of the Generation Y while 33%, mostly the older ones, considered themselves part of the older Generation X. This means that many of them are behaving like their parents in Generation X!

Generation Z (+1995) – under eighteen. Global warming, economic crisis, Arab revolution, Cloud computing, mobile everywhere, tablet natives, WhatsApp and Snapchat. They are technonerds and technology savvy, with gadgets and the newest toys. Their world is digital, they expect speed. They are in the middle of the digital revolution and transformation, and are still in their formative years so it's too early to tell how they'll turn out. The current fears for this generation are the recession, climate change, refugees, terrorists and politics. They will be critical, conservative, look for certainty, expect a new realism as they are realists. They communicate with images[77] and love streaming video and music. They are called streaming natives with half of the 16 to 18-year-old spending more than one hour on YouTube per day. They are future focused. They'll say yes to smart choices, yes to norm-core (normal), yes to traditional values, for example they don't want the age of consensual sex to go down.

Hannah Scurfield, Research Director Intel, says, 'They will value honesty, transparency and have a very direct relationship with brands.' They are digital natives at heart, the tech-innates that use five screens at once.

Generation Z have what's being called a highly evolved 'eight-second filter.'[78] It's not they have little focus, or can only pay attention for eight seconds; it's that with all the distractions they have, with the thousands of messages and bytes of data thrown at them, they have learned to be selective. If you don't interest them in eight seconds, they move on.

By 2020, Millennials[79] or Generation Y will be half the global workforce, and in the US this will go up to 75%, meaning the expectations of the Millennials will influence how companies are run and organised.

	Silent Generation	Baby Boomers
	Pre-1945	1945-1960
Wars	WW II	Cold War Start Vietnam
Events	Many political & civil rights leaders Great depression 1930	Woodstock Sex, drugs, rock&roll Swinging sixties Moonlanding JFK / Martin Luther King assassination Baby boom post WW II
Love	Cars	TV MTV First computers
Family	Fix gender roles Family focus	Family not first priority Me-generation Cult of the child
Feeling	Scared	Questions authority Rejection traditional values
Career	For life Hard workers Job security	Job security
Money	Save	On credit Increased consumerism
Technology	Car	Phone – TV
Communication	Letter	Phone – email
Digital	Ignorant or disengaged	Mix Ignorant – Early adopters

Generation X	Generation Y Millenials	Generation Z iGeneration
1961-1980	1981-1995	Post- 1995
End cold war End Vietnam Yugoslavia Last Soviet children	Iraq 9/11 War on terror	Terrorism Syria ISIS
Pollution Thatcher & Reaganomics Post-boomers Birth control pill Sexual revolution	Economic crash late 2000 Third Industrial Revolution	Global warming, Arab revolution, Cloud & mobile Fourth Industrial Revolution
PC Everything in 2s: cars, TV, ...	Gaming console, Internet, Social networks, Phone remote control to digital	Mobile devices Whatsap, Instagram, Virtual Reality, 3D printing, Tablets
Work-life balance Increased divorces Cult of the adult	Generation We New boomers Live&work in urban areas Living with parents	Yes to norm-core Traditional values Honesty
Cynical Independent	Skeptical about religion, banks and politics Narcissists/special 33% feel part of Generation Y Optimists	Formative years Fear for recession, climate change, refuges, terrorists & politics Realists
Both working	Work with and not for organization Startup Self-development Discovery	Open-minded Freelancing Fast & Furious Learning Purpose Success
Conservative	Earn to spend	Crowd-sourcing
PC – TV	PC-Tablets-smartphones 2 screens	Tablets-Smartphones Up to 5 screens
email – SMS	SMS – social media	Skype/Facetime Mobile device 8 second generation Video, Images
Switched-on Savvy	Natives	Nerds Tablet natives

Source Mary Keener Internet Trend Report 2016,
https://en.wikipedia.org/wiki/Generation#List_of_generations, Olivier Van Duüren

So the older you are, the more likely it is that a phone call would be a good way to connect with you, but if you're younger, the last thing you want is a phone call. The best way will be social and chat.

Before the global financial crisis of 2008, considered by many to have been the worst financial crisis since the Great Depression of the 1930s, in many ways the ideal path for a youngster's career was for them to join a bank, a top consulting firm or one of the big tech companies. After the crash, many of them lost their jobs. The new generation who were ending their studies saw what was happening around them and realised that job safety wasn't guaranteed any more. So many, combined with the strength and accessibility of new Cloud enabled technologies, started a new job or a first job as an entrepreneur, becoming one of the main reasons for the start-up influx. This generation of entrepreneurs is used to working in chaotic, super-fast, fluid test-and-learn environments in everything they do, at home or at work. They are not tuned for long-term planning as their brains are focused on the fast and the furious. They look for adventure, using the incredible platform of learning and self-development.

While classification by age group is great, the following will also influence where you land: life cycle stages, because you can be thirty-two, unmarried and living with your parents, or thirty-two with your own home, married, with three kids, and mindset. You might belong to one generation by age, but have a mindset that is part of another generation.

So, it is not so much your age as your mindset. You can have a Millennial mindset and be a Generation X age member. This means that there will be generational differences in the workspace changing the dynamics of work. Digital savvy younger workers will need to work with the play-by-the-rules way of some older employees. Understanding these differences is critical so you can create the optimal conditions for the right communication and work health. All employees need to feel they are respected for who they are, what they like and how they can contribute to the bigger purpose of the company. Each generation has slightly different core values and their expectations are formed by important events that took place in their life span.

What will be next? Maybe we could call the next generation the Generation D or the Dualarity Generation for those making personal and business transformations by seeing and energising themselves.

Ageing society

So we have a blend of generations meeting each other, and with rapid evolution in biological, technological and medical sciences, people are living longer, meaning a growing part of the population will need to be taken care of. By 2050 we will have more than 2 billion people aged over 60 on our planet, twice the number of today. How do we keep employment high enough for the ageing population so they can be part of the economic system as long as they need to be?

Global life expectancy is increasing at a fast speed:[80] the global average was forty-seven years in 1950, sixty-nine years in 2014, and estimates are that in 2050 it will be seventy-six years. With this, the proportion of elderly is increasing both in advanced (from 14% over sixty-five in 2000 to 26% in 2050) and emerging (from 5% over sixty-five in 2000 to 14% in 2050) economies. The share of older workers (fifty-five+) will increase dramatically from 14% in 2010 to 22% in 2030. Without real productivity gains and increases, GDP (gross domestic product) growth will shrink substantially. Employment and the future of work will be a dominant factor for our future growth, as long as the employment gives people a level of fulfilment and value.

The main demographic trends are of slowing overall world population growth,[81] +1.2% versus +2% in 1975, with slowing birth rates, down 39% since 1960, and rising lifespans at seventy-two years, up 36% since 1960.

The gender gap

The gender gap will increase again after a few years of progress as it is female dominated jobs that are more likely to be automated. The WEF Global Gender Report 2015[82] believes that at the current pace it will take 118 years before equality is reached, and this might be impacted even more by future automation.

Healthcare

Today there are more than 23,000 mobile applications related to health, and these are driven by mobile innovations, wearables, changing demographics and related cost pressure. The availability of big data and AI makes it possible to have real-time insights with focus on a healthy life, prevention and real-time analytics. The demand for a healthy life and getting the right insight and suggested actions will be one of the main powers of change in managing the health of people.

The future is already here – it's just not evenly distributed.
William Gibson

Geopolitical Instability

The Internal Displacement Monitoring Center[83] (IDMC) found more than 40.8 million people were on the run from their own country in December 2015. During 2015 more than 27.8 million additional people were displaced in 127 countries due to conflict, violence and disasters. These displacements were driven in the Middle-East and Africa by the Arabic Revolution and the rise of ISIS, and mean that beyond blending generations, cultures are being blended, with high society impacts which will influence how a country and its society will thrive in the digital transformation.

They have also impacted on the political landscape, especially in Europe with the UK debating and voting on Brexit (to leave the EU) and right wing parties gaining voters in multiple countries due to the economic crisis, from which Europe still hasn't recovered. The European project has lost believers, which has had implications in all countries where people are taking a stand for the left or right wing and are demanding a change in politics.

In Austria in 2016 the presidential seat was won by an extreme left winger with just a couple of per cent more votes than an extreme right wing candidate. In the US Donald Trump and Bernie Sanders, a political Dualarity, are mobilising a new type of political movement of those who want to see change and oppose the current political order. Theirs is an anti-establishment fight with Washington DC as the main target and the Clintons representing the old order. The same happened in the UK where 52% voted to leave the EU during the Brexit referendum in June 2016 – a referendum against the current establishment and Brussels as the heart of the EU. Brexit divided the country in two with two bad councils named fear and hate, and the results were: United Kingdom = Divided Kingdom; United Generations = Divided Generations as 64% of the eighteen-to twenty-four-year-olds voted for the remain camp while less than 35% of those above fifty voted to stay in the EU. United Europe = Divided Europe. And this is all feeding the ScotExit with Scotland wanting to leave the UK, Marine Le Pen with Frexit in France, Geert Wilders with Nexit in the Netherlands, ItalExit in Italy, and Fixit with Finland struggling most with the Russian embargo. These are all creating a divide between generations, cities, countries, and adding severe economic risks to the Dualarity of the world of peace and order.

Dualarity Of Globalisation

Fast growing economies and emerging markets like Asia and Africa are accelerating to meet the needs and demands from the growing middle-class. Emerging markets are still expected to see strong growth, driven by India with over 7% and China with more than 6%.[84] The Philippines, Kenya, India and Indonesia grew more than 5% in 2015. Many start-ups and businesses with innovative platforms are trying to answer that middle-class need, while large incumbents are struggling to determine their responding strategies.

> The world economy's operating system is being rewritten.
>
> **Richard Dobbs, James Manyika, and Jonathan Woetzel,**
> *No Ordinary Disruption*

The upcoming innovations and possibilities are significant. The question may be what this means from an economic point of view, and as Dani Rodrik, Turkish economist and Ford Foundation Professor of International Political Economy at the John F. Kennedy School of Government at Harvard University, remarks, 'Not only for the top, the happy few, but for the whole global economy.'[85] This could engage big parts of the economy.

According to MGI (McKinsey Global Institute's)[86] latest report, the global flows of volume in trade, finance, people and data are increasing and today contribute between 250 billion and 450 billion to the yearly GDP (gross domestic product is a monetary measure of the market value of all final goods and services produced in a year). MGI's analysis finds that over a decade, world GDP has risen by 10.1% over what would have resulted in a world without any cross-border business. The latest MGI Connectedness Index finds large gaps between a few leading countries and the rest of the world. Singapore is leading the latest rankings, followed by the Netherlands, the United States and Germany, with advanced economies remaining more connected than developing countries.

We have seen multiple industrial revolutions, and the first three changed fundamentally how we live, providing electricity, cars and the internet, and the changes were both on the demand and the supply side. Supply skills mapped rather well with the consumption. It took decades to see the impact, which is not the case today with the current digital revolution. There is a skills gap between innovation and supply as only countries that are connected and on the road to digital transformation have the skills to develop, so the benefits of driverless cars, for example, might not add a lot to global economy. Right now it's hard to predict the impact on the global economy in the statistics, so we might want to wait a few decades. In general, more globalisation is considered good, but there is no guarantee that everyone will be better off.

Since the speed of the go-to market is increasing, it is important for many companies in the digital global economy to re-evaluate their entire supply chain. Our generation is an on-demand one that wants it now. According to a recent UPS survey, approximately one-third of high-tech companies are moving their manufacturing or assembly closer to end-user markets[87] to speed up the connection between order, production and delivery. The adoption of 3D printing could impact the whole manufacturing value chains and change where companies are basing their production. Our energy needs will increase by 33% in 2030. There is a need for $420 billion in investments in efficient and renewable energy. Some believe that we could solve our energy concerns by exploiting Mars and other planets in the near future. In the UK, Japanese car manufacturer Nissan and the Italian energy company Enel are joining forces to produce hundreds of Nissan cars and trucks systems that will give back battery energy, and earn money with it, to address this growing demand. Tesla already has a home battery called Tesla Powerwall.

The power of China on the global economy and its acquisition hunger is growing by the minute. In 2016 it will reach a staggering 300 billion euros, up from less than 60 billion in 2010. The many Chinese state companies have too much cash which they are using to invest in companies around the world in all sectors, from entertainment, oil, electricity, hotels to football clubs like Inter Milan. The Chinese prime-minister, Li Keqiang, said he would expect an additional $1,000 billion investment in foreign acquisitions in the next five years.[88] The potential acquisition for 4.6 billion euros of a German company Kuka, one of the most known industrial robot companies, by the Chinese Midea group is creating a huge amount of attention and getting German politics involved to protect its industrial assets.

To paraphrase fellow of Oxford Martin School Christopher Kutarna's post 'There's never been a better time to be alive. So why the globalization backlash?': life expectancy has risen by more than fifty years in the last 1,000 years, one-eighth of humanity lives in poverty versus more than two-fifths when the Berlin Wall fell, and global illiteracy has declined to one-sixth in the same time frame. We live healthier, wealthier, better and more digitally connected than any other time in our history. However, middle-class salaries have stagnated, extreme poverty has increased, we've never felt so vulnerable, and in many cases, fear dominates. We are being asked to live in a complex world full of transformation with major global challenges upon us.

We will need to live in this Dualarity of globalisation, to act and find energy to solve problems step by step, turning around rock by rock. And we will need to do it together.

Society And Industry Implications

Whether we like it or not, the future is coming. We can waste a lot of energy fighting it or we can put our energy into helping our next society and industry to thrive. The future is our new home, so let's be inspired by it while we learn fast from our mistakes, set some rules to maximise what is coming and minimise the nasty side-effects. Politics and government[89] will play a role, but this is probably already bigger than them. Understanding what is happening by seeing and looking around us is a critical step.

So what does this mean for our society and industry? What are the implications? In the next section we will be looking at a selection of them.[90]

If the world were 100 people.[91]

50 would be female 50 would be male	31 Christians 21 Muslims 16 non-religious 14 Hindus 12 other religion 6 Buddhists	1 college education 1 owns computer
20 would be children 66 would be adults 14 would be 65 and older	52 speak other languages 17 Chinese dialect 8 Hindustani 8 English 7 Spanish 4 Arabic 4 Russian	75 have food and shelter 25 would not 83 have access to safe drinking water
61 Asian 14 Western Hemisphere 13 Africans 12 Europeans	82 can read and write 18 can't	1 dying by starvation 17 from undernourished 15 from overweight

Source www.100people.org

Let's take a look at the worldwide population.[92] Today there are 7.2 billion people on this planet, the urbanised area is around 50%, and around 3.4 billion of those people are active internet users. There are 2 billion active social media accounts, 3.6 billion unique mobile users. Hundreds of millions of people are using their mobile phone to call and make micro payments, even though they don't have a smartphone. They don't have the internet. In Africa, countries like Kenya are leading the way in using mobile phones to make payments.

If we look at the internet penetration around the world, it's diverse: in North America it is around 90%, Western Europe around 80%, but in the Middle East, only 35% have internet, with just 26% in Africa. So Western Europe and North America are leading the way with internet penetration, while more than 4 billion people have no access to internet today. There are a lot of initiatives taking place to enhance the accessibility for the rest of the world, but around 1.2 billion people don't even have electricity.

Elon Musk, with Space X, is sending four thousand satellites up in the next five years. Alphabet Inc. (Google) has Project Loon, using hundreds of helium balloons that will be closer to the earth, meaning better reception.[93] Richard Branson, Coca Cola and Qualcomm have combined their efforts in the OneWeb satellite initiative planned for 2019, and the O3b Networks have twelve satellites. Experts are predicting that 90% of the entire population will be connected to the internet within ten years.

Microsoft and Facebook have agreed to build a 6,600km subsea cable jointly, called Marea,[94] designed to carry 160 terabytes of data per second (1 terabyte = 1000 gigabytes) across the Atlantic Ocean to meet the growing demand for high-speed Cloud, bandwidth and online services. It is expected to be completed by the end of 2017 and will connect the United States with southern Europe. The move comes nearly two years after Alphabet Inc.

agreed with five Asian companies to invest about $300 million to develop and operate a trans-Pacific cable network connecting the United States to Japan. Google either has or plans to invest in five undersea cables, Microsoft four, Facebook two and Amazon one.

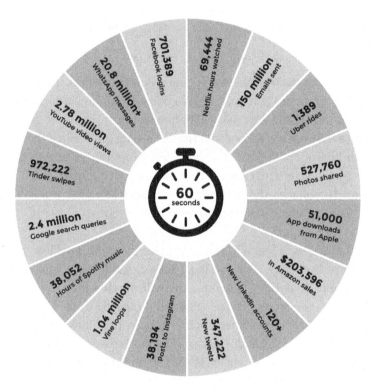

Source Excelacom 2016

If we look at a typical internet minute around the world: 2.4 million Google searches are performed, 2.7 million videos are viewed, 293,000 statuses are updated, 104,000 Skype calls are made and 122,000 Instagram images are posted. Just imagine the data that this represents. The abundance is unbelievable. Big data is here, and the data produced by businesses is doubling every 1.2 years.

If we look to 2020, we'll go from 6.4 billion devices to 50 billion connected devices because of the invisible industrial revolution. The amount of data that these will produce will be massive. We will go from 2.6 billion smartphones to 6.1 billion smartphones. We'll probably have around 250,000 IoT enabled driverless cars in production. We'll have more than 10 million items of smart clothing. Digital will represent 25% of the worldwide economy, and will become an $11 trillion business by 2025.

What is more important is the change in the labour force. Generation Y will be 50% of the future workforce in 2025. Generation Z (the eight second generation) will become 30% of the workforce in 2030, which means that by 2040 more than 60% of the workforce will be digital natives (Generations Y and Z).

Welcome To The Industrial Revolution 4.0

> Listen, the next revolution is gonna be a revolution of ideas.
>
> **Bill Hicks**

When we see the changes that are taking place, we can see we are on the verge of the Industrial Revolution 4.0. There has been a lot of debate about whether it is a fourth revolution or an extension of the third revolution, but most agree by now that we have entered a new one; that it is the digital revolution bridging the human with the cyber world.

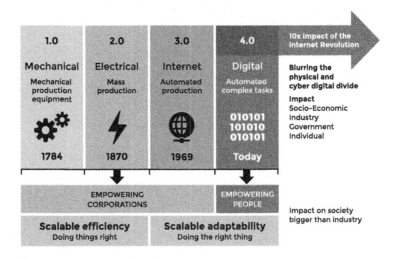

If we look at the image, we see three major industrial revolutions that have taken place through history. The Industrial Revolution 1.0 was the mechanical revolution, centred around production of equipment powered and driven by water and steam. We had the first mechanical looms introduced in 1784. The Second Industrial

Revolution occurred in 1870, the phase of the electrical revolution. Mass production was enabled by division of labour and the use of electrical energy. The first assembly line, the Ford line, was probably the most famous example, but perhaps less well-known are the Cincinnati slaughterhouse lines. These first revolutions were only scalable by adding bodies – they relied on humans to achieve more. They were scale-efficient by doing things right.

The Third Industrial Revolution occurred in 1969, with the advent of micro-controllers and IT automating manufacturing, and when the internet was launched. The internet came from the military, from ARPANET, and was designed to keep military communications going when the phone system was down. This was then further developed by two computer scientists, the Belgian, Robert Cailliau, and a Brit, Tim Berners-Lee, into what we know today as the World Wide Web. This revolution was scalable: add more computers, IT systems and technology, and improve scalability. By doing the right thing we could achieve economies of scale.

The Fourth Industrial Revolution is distinguishable from the third because it is where humans meet the cyber world; where technology and people are not distinct, not separate. We had the PC and we had a life – today our devices and sensors will become an extension of us. Facebook is an extension of us. Our phones are extensions of us. Our smart watches are extensions of who we are and what we do. This fourth revolution has the same triggers as the third revolution, but it's cyber meets human this time.

It's the same in businesses. Everything gets integrated, customised and smart-automated. The Industrial Revolution 4.0 automates complex tasks; it's the age of the Internet Of Things and Cloud computing. Where the first three revolutions were mainly about empowering organisations, almost all innovation in the last few years has been driven by the consumer and is now changing organisations from the inside.

When we look at the changes that are taking place, the next revolution will be in an invisible world. So far the three main revolutions have all been very visible. We could see the tablets, the iPhones, the wearables – they were visible, but increases in our capabilities are powered by technology that moves further out of sight, becomes invisible. Innovation will come from the shift to the Cloud – invisible processing power, storage, intelligence. More innovation will come from what's happening inside and around the device versus the object we can see – artificial intelligence, powerful algorithms, Cloud computing. An ecosystem of computing will surround us, becoming so natural it will disappear into the background. Less intrusive, it will fit into more parts of our world and solve more problems. User interfaces will become integrated and we will control them with voice, gaze, gesture. We will see the results, not the effort.

> It is time to understand it – and not as a curiosity or an entry in the annals of technology or business but as an integral part of our humanity, as the latest and most powerful extension and expression of the project of being human.
>
> **Virginia Heffernan,** *Magic and Loss: The Internet as Art*

Virginia Heffernan believes that the internet is a great masterpiece of human civilisation rivalling the pyramids, agriculture or monotheism. Possibly not everyone would agree.

There are at least three differences between Industrial Revolution 4.0 and the previous ones:

1 Speed – this revolution is upon us rapidly
2 Pervasiveness – it's about mobile networks, sensors, nanotechnology, brain research, computing, networks, etc. being accessible and affordable
3 Entirety – it is creating the global shared economy.

We will have an empowered ecosystem of consumers and enterprises that are the Dualarity. Four evolutions, driven by the physical, digital, and biological worlds, will have an impact on our economy, business, government, society and the individual, with distinct opportunities and challenges.

> We stand on the brink of a technological revolution that will fundamentally alter the way we live, work, and relate to one another. In its scale, scope, and complexity, the transformation will be unlike anything humankind has experienced before.
>
> Klaus Schwab, President of the World Economic Forum,
> *The Fourth Industrial Revolution*

Our current model and the new model are not fluently integrating with each other, and yes, there will be casualties along the way – those who are being disrupted by the dynamics of the new world and those who lack the ability to adapt and adjust – a Dualarity.

Some researchers say that the comprehensive nature and scale of the cataclysm of physical, digital and biological world changes coming together will be transformational. The majority of the government ecosystem is built upon models with mostly national rules, national taxes, local hiring and salary taxes to pay social security. The Industrial Revolution 4.0 is disrupting this model and the notion of being national is getting a different meaning. Of course, ethical questions, similar to the debates around the use of atomic energy and genetic research, will need to be answered as this connected super-intelligent world evolves, and new playing rules will need to reflect those questions.

The best technologies are the ones that you stop noticing.

Chris Thorn, British Heart Foundation

New Samsung fridges provide us with the capability to scan the barcodes of products as we place them in the fridge and when we take them out. The fridge will then recommend items for ordering and can do it online for us, if we want. There are screens we can place on the wall or windows that we can project on to. Everything will become integrated into the environment; there will be natural ways of controlling things through voice, gesture, emotion, touches, and they will anticipate our needs and enhance our lives. Our lives will follow us as we walk through the walls.

Bill Gates, in his house in Seattle, has technology that knows who his guests are when they arrive. It defines what kind of art and music they like, and when they walk through the corridors, the paintings change. If they like classical music, they are accompanied by classical music. In the coming years, all houses will personalise experiences for every visitor, and of course for us. If the house computer knows that at 9pm a person likes cosy lights for reading, it will give them cosy lights. It will recognise through cameras in their house that they're reading and sitting down with a glass of wine, probably wine ordered by the Samsung fridge.

A Transformation Centred On Digital

> We do not need magic to transform our world. We carry all the power we need inside ourselves already.
>
> J.K. Rowling

There are three main interconnected and immutable things to consider when looking at what the digital transformation means to our businesses. One is putting the customer at the heart. The second is seeing digital as the oxygen, and the third is recognising people as the soul. We have seen these pillars before; they go through everything we do as a person and as a business.

This digital transformation is changing every business by technological and/or business model innovation into a digital business. Instead of being an enterprise that uses digital, businesses need to become digital enterprises. This transformation impacts the foundational elements of businesses, and the three pillars have to be aligned to the company's overarching why and what. Why is your company doing what it does? What are you doing? This is a strategy.

We can imagine the three pillars in a different way: the customer at the heart is B2C (business to consumers), putting our customers at the heart of everything we do; digital as the oxygen is all about the business model B2B or B2C – an operating model, value chain, new business models, entrepreneurship, start-ups, everything is in there. Then we have the new people architecture – people as the soul is about B2E, business to employees. All of these align to a company's why (B2Y) and what (B2W).

The rise of digital natives is changing the demographics of organisations. With the changing demographics, we have more connected collaborators and engaged employees, and this engagement and collaboration goes across hierarchies centred around projects. They are an HR rebirth where we need to provide a workplace that is good for the digital natives as well as the incumbent population (the digital immigrants). It's not about replacing the incumbents with millennials, it's about helping them both to craft a mindset that takes everyone along on the journey. This requires cultural and leadership attribute changes, which we'll look at later.

Many roles within organisations and the dynamics between employer and employee are changing. We are seeing chief digital officers taking leadership roles, chief marketing officers becoming more digitalised and potentially merging with the CIO (chief innovation officer). How do we blend the roles? What is the ideal profile we need to lead the change?

This also has personal disruption implications for each of our employees. Should we move from static hierarchies to dynamic hierarchies that are more organised around projects? We will see multiple evolutions of the management structures as we move ahead.

There is a battle for talent recruitment and retention. Those companies that continue to use old technology and operate on a fixed mindset will struggle to recruit young talent and will be in danger of losing their incumbents. Technology innovation is expected in the office; lack of innovation inside the company, outdated culture and slow pace of adoption will strangle companies. Training and education will become more important, companies and individuals will have to become proactive, and we need to define how we will be proactive. The challenge that every company will see is that they need to balance performing and transforming. Every individual has to carry on doing what they did before, and they will need to change with the company. Performing while transforming will become the new normal, and we transform ourselves before we transform others.

> In the past culture was an option in transformation and only came into play once the performing was complete. Today performance, behavioural change and culture are part of one transformational project. All three in the digital transformation era now have to be in balance at the same time if you want to transform faster.
>
> **Michel Van der Bel, President Microsoft EMEA**

Real Madrid is a perfect case of digital transformation which had people at the heart, in this case the fans. Microsoft worked with **Real Madrid** to help it transform its business. The club had a turnover of $700 million on everything it sold and 450 million worldwide fans. Cristiano Ronaldo is the most followed person on this planet with more than 111 million fans, and when the well-known French management school INSEAD researched the impact of sportsmen on social media, it found that Ronaldo personifies the ideal mix to have maximum impact: information, interaction and inspiration. Just watch how he stole all attention during the European Championship final against France. Despite being injured after twenty-five minutes, he inspired his team from the sidelines to win with their heart. Which they did and Ronaldo was their hero.

Real Madrid overall is the number one sports franchise in the world. However, it discovered that it didn't know its fans very well. It knew it had a huge number of fans, but it didn't know where the majority were living and who they were. When it compared itself with clubs like Manchester United, it realised it wasn't making the best use of it asset: the fans. Manchester United was able to connect and engage with its fans, ultimately raising more revenue per fan.

Real Madrid developed a trajectory of fans, a social listening system, discovering where the fans were and what they were saying about the club. It's like a big screen projected on to a wall with a map of the world, where coloured lights appear when anyone is talking about the club or posts something around Ronaldo. It captures social listening, who and where. It uncovered that the biggest fan base is in Indonesia, with 34–35 million. It even found a small island in the Pacific Ocean that has one fan, and each time the club says something about Real, he lights up on the island. Real Madrid learned so much, but it was also fun, and then it started working on changing the whole customer fan experience to reach the fans not only when they are in the stadium, but before and after. Unique experiences encourage fans to come to the stadium not only half an hour before the match, like fans do in most European countries, but maybe three hours before because they want to be there. The club looked for ways to provide unique experiences for different time zones where people can't follow the game live. It gave specific access to the training ground to allow fans to see what was happening in the catacombs of Real Madrid. Everything was redesigned; it hired a designer to draw experiences in an artistic way, looking from the perspective of a fan.

Then it looked at the skill set it had internally. Two hundred people were the soul of the organisation, and they all needed bringing along on the journey. Job descriptions and training got a reboot. The club didn't only add more digital people, it trained everyone to be more savvy using digital.

The process with Real Madrid started with B2C (business to consumer), or B2F (business to fan) in its case, all about building a digital experience for the fans. It then moved to B2B to bring sponsors onboard, monetising everything it did, giving more access, leveraging assets, giving sponsors access to the fans in a very sophisticated way while respecting the privacy of the fans. Food, ticketing and sponsoring all needed to be redefined in the digital space.

This change also redefined the why. Why was Real Madrid doing what it did? It realised it was transitioning from a sports company to a media and entertainment company. By redefining the why and what of Real Madrid, Microsoft helped it transition from a mature sports company to a healthy media company.

This is an ongoing process at all levels, with people as the soul, digital as the oxygen and the customer, the fans, at the heart, and a platform to monetise and grow as a business.

> It is [the most] complete disruption of the business model that football has had over the past 15 to 20 years.
>
> **José Ángel Sánchez, CEO Real Madrid**

Real Madrid redesigned its business model, and others are following. Around the world, people are looking at what Real Madrid is doing; the club's estimated by Forbes to be worth around $3.5 billion, making it the richest club in the world.

Disrupted Industries

Companies like Uber and Airbnb, powered by the Cloud, have disrupted traditional business models. They are for sure the Uber cases of digital disruption. This has fuelled more disruptors and start-ups to reimagine businesses. Traditional businesses are vulnerable to this Cloud disruption[95] and are trying to own their digital future. For some it is more likely they will be disrupted by digitisation in general than be Uberised as such.

As presented at the Industry Cloud Forum 2015 by Capital Keynote,[96] we see at one side the enablers who sell services powered by the Cloud working with the existing industry model, and on the other side we see the disruptors building entire new offerings and disrupting the existing industry models, often giving consumers direct connection to providers. They have the talent, look more and more like software companies, and claim they honestly want to change the lives of their customers and employees for the better.

Industry	Enablers	Disrupters
Transportation	Dache (China), Drivewyze, Flywheel, Hailo, Kuaidi, Whisk	Lyft, Sidecar, Uber
Finance & Mortgages	Advent Software, Blend Labs, nCino, Plaid, PrecisionLender	Betterment, Lending Clubm Lendinghome, OnDeck, Square, Wealthfront
Insurance	Ebix Inc, Guidewire, Navera, Solera Holdings	Oscar, Zenefits, Zen99
Law Enforcement	InterAct, Mark43, Shotspotter	Bannermen
Real Estate	Apto, CoStar, Hightower, Honest Buildings, Nestio, Realpage, Viewthespace	Compass, Houwzer, Liquid Spaces, WeWork, Zenly, Zillow

Industry	Enablers	Disrupters
Logistics	Fleetmatics, Keep Truckin, Lanetix	Dispatcher,Cargomatic, Flexport
Legal	Clio, Everlaw, Judicate, Lex Machina, Ravel	Lawdingo, RocketLawyer, Upcouncsel
Hospitality (Hotels)	Alice App	Airbnb, Hotel Tonight
Energy/Utilities	EnerNoc, Opower, Tachyus	Faraday, SolarCity, Stern, Tesla
Agriculture	Climate Corporation, Rainwave, Solum	Ceres Imaging, Conservis, DroneDeploy, Farmers's Business Network, Granular
Education	Blackboard, ClassDojo, Clever, Civitas Learning, Edmodo, Nearpod, Top Hat, 2U	Coursera, Khan Academy, Fedora
Healthcare/Life Sciences	Athenahealth, Augmedix, Doximity, MedeAnalytics, Medidata, Veeva	Doctor on Demand, One Medical Group, Medicast, Zocdoc
Construction	Autodesk, BuildingConnected, Fieldwire, Fieldlens, Plangrid, Procore, Textura	Getable, VaiVolta, Komatsu, Winsun

Source Emergence Capital Partners

Let us now zoom into some industries in disruption or changing at a high speed, starting with the **media and entertainment industry** where music and video watching seems to be going through a major change. Personalisation, engagement and delivering content at the right moment and in the right context will underpin the digital transformation in this sector. As one of the first industries being impacted by the early stages of the digital revolution it has gone through multiple waves of innovation like the internet, mobile and social. And today, with the massive explosion of available content distributed all over the place, it faces new challenges around how to connect it all, create the content and monetise assets in the best way.

Is the **music download industry** coming to an end? The music industry went through a huge change with the introduction of Apple's iTunes store in 2003, post the illegal download industry with the likes of Napster. ITunes allows you to make unlimited downloads of music to your iPod for a small fee per month. With the smartphone came music streaming sites such as Spotify[97] with 30 million paying fans which reached 100 million users in May 2016. Music downloads accounted for \$3.9billion turnover in Apple's heyday in 2012, or three-quarters of the total digital music sales, but by 2019 the iTunes revenue will only be \$600million. Apple music tried to launch a streaming service with 'only' 13 million paying fans. This shows that a freemium economic model like Spotify, free and funded by subscription or advertising, is the way to go in the online world.

Video streaming services like Amazon Prime, Netflix and Hulu are changing the way we consume content through video. Facebook contracted 140 content media companies worth \$50million, such as NY Times, Buzzfeed, The Huffington Post, and celebrities such as Gordon Ramsay or American Football star Russell Wilson, the aim being to entertain 1.65 billion Facebook users with great content through Facebook Life, its streaming services. The average Facebook user watches eight videos a day, so Facebook Life aims to capture a larger share of the video advertising market and compete with contenders like Twitter, Snapchat, and especially YouTube. Netflix, Amazon Instant Video and Oculus Rift "Sleepy Hollow" received dozens of Emmy nominations. And platforms like HBO Now, Sling TV, Netflix and Hulu are part of a larger paradigm shift, in terms of how and when consumers want to consume content. This will further impact the business model of the traditional broadcasters and telco players.

In **retail,** let us take a look at what is happening in the fight for domination between the retail giants Amazon, pure play e-commerce, and Walmart, the biggest off-line retailer in the world.

In 2012 Walmart had a turnover of $444billion, more than sixteen times higher than Amazon. It was the third most valuable American company and global retailer, employing a staggering 2.2 million people over 11,500 stores in twenty-eight countries around the world. In 2016 Amazon's market cap of $331.6billion surpassed Walmart's $219billion by more than $100billion. Walmart's online e-commerce business has a long way to go, still only representing a tiny piece of its turnover. As Mintel (www.mintel.com) shows, 'only' 33% of US shoppers shop online each week, and with these statistics in hand Walmart probably thinks it has some time. While Amazon is expanding its remit and testing delivery with drones, Walmart has a way to go. Fortune 500 shows that Walmart in 2015 had a $482billion turnover with a $15billion profit, while Amazon had a $107billion revenue with a small profit of $215million. Why? Because Amazon is putting all its profit into new innovations, and this is exactly why it is so disruptive. It continuously introduces new value to the customer, redefining the retail experience, becoming the standard of what customers expect in retail, which has an impact on Walmart's strategy. Walmart needs to adjust to stay relevant.

This is the difference between an offensive and defensive strategy; between healthy and mature where, in this case, the mature company is getting injured.

Digital dis-intermediation is a big threat clearly visible in the **financial technology world, Fintech.** The whole finance industry is being disrupted by technology, with the Bitcoin currency collaboration platform Blockchain removing many parts of banking's middle layers and putting the authority of a bank at stake. In simple words, today you can wire money from one bank account to another in a second versus two or more days. Tech giants are launching their own mobile payment services like Apple Pay, Samsung Pay, Google/Android pay, forcing banks to merge and connect the digital and branch experiences while visitors to branches decline. Banking today is a long-term gamble as it's becoming a very crowded and competitive world with uncertain future outcomes.

China's giants in the financial technology world have emerged beyond being super strong disruptors.

> The BAT – the search giant Baidu, Alibaba Aliplay service owning 80% of all Chinese mobile payment and Tencent chat application used by more than 500 million people, including payments and wealth management – are leading the Chinese wave of disruption in financial services, making deeper inroads than their western counterparts.
>
> **Haydn Shaughnessy, Co-Founder of advisory firm The Disruption House, and Zennon Kapron, Director at market research firm Kapronasia**

In pursuit of becoming digital,[98] western banks have focused on platform updates, partnerships and acquisitions and, most recently, Blockchain. But will these strategies be enough against China's competition?

The **transportation** sector, defined as the connected traveller, autonomous driving and the digital ecosystem surrounding the automotive industry, will suffer the most from the technological revolution, as we will see in the next section. We have the impact of Uber, the American multinational online transportation network company, on the whole taxi business and on the notion of transporting something. In 2016 Uber was present in more than 300 cities in sixty countries, providing more than 1 million rides a day, adding 50,000 new drivers a month and creating 150,000 jobs. Uber is now testing self-driving cars in collaboration with Ford Fusion in Pennsylvania, the goal being to reduce costs by eliminating the driver and increase safety on the road (90% of car accidents are due to human error). Uber has had a vast impact on all industries as it has shown, like Netflix, Airbnb and Apple TV, that one platform can change a whole industry, and it's displacing other traditional business models as it launches UberEAT, UberPOOL and Uber Lease. Governments and the traditional transport sector are reacting by trying to ban Uber where they can, mostly without success, or by filing more than 180 lawsuits.

The renewable and storage **energy** industry is changing rapidly, driven by energy storage leaders, like Tesla's Powerwall and Powerpack in the US, the German market leader Sonnen and Japan's Panasonic Smart Towns,[99] currently delivering solutions and starting to scale. On 15 May 2016 Germany was able to see, for the first time, 99% of its energy needs supplied with renewable energy such as sun, wind, biomass and hydroenergy.[100]

The **manufacturing** industry is deeply transforming through multiple disruptive powers like big data analytics, machine learning, Internet of Things, 3D printing, automation like robotics and vehicles, and new materials. This will impact how products are designed, manufactured and used, with the spoils going to those who put the customer at the heart, understanding their needs and building the factories of the future where a product becomes a full service.[101]

Healthcare is on the verge of being redefined completely. People will have a video e-consultation, receive self-diagnoses prescribed by their mobile app, Google search or wearable, and have new medical tools at their fingertips – a more connected e-relationship between consumers and the health professionals.

Creation Of New Customer Archetypes

Humanity will change more in the next 20 years than in all of human history.

Futurist, Gerd Leonhard

The Industrial Revolution 4.0 and the pace of adoption has created new customer digital archetypes – the digital consumer, the digital citizen and the digital enterprise. Along with those we have the digital network and the legacy consumer and enterprise, and digital immigrants.

We will now look at the three archetypes.

The digital consumer

As we saw in the previous section, for the digital customers there are three different stages of adoption of technology:

1 **Digital natives** are digital fluent, always on. They thrive on social sites, play around with new tools; they grew up with digital at their fingertips. They are mostly Generation Y, the millennials, and the technology innate Generation Z, and they are frequently in the healthy quadrant of the Dualarity
2 **Digital savvy** are those people who were not born with digitalisation but have adopted it because they see the value of it. They use social, read newspapers on a tablet, have stopped printing photos and now share them by Facebook or email, and they have transposed their offline world to the online world. Baby Boomers and Generation X will be here. You will often find them in the mature quadrant of the Dualarity
3 **Digital ignorants** are still living in the offline world. They don't trust anything online, they use phones to make calls, or at best

send an SMS, they read a printed newspaper and they have a television in the corner of the room. They may not have adopted technology because they are scared, feel it is too complex or they don't have an interest. They prefer how it was in the old days. Most of the Silent Generation and some Baby Boomers are here. These people will either fall into the scared or injured quadrants.

This third group might test new things out, but only because they *need* to, not because they want to. They might get a wrist band with health information included, or they want their kids to be safe so they use an app for monitoring them, or they might use a Zembro (https://www.zembro.com/uk-EN/) button for elderly people so if they fall they have a safety net.

These three types have their needs and wants to be addressed, without assumptions. With the vast networks available and the huge amounts of data, assumption is redundant; you can ask them what they want.

The digital citizen and their government

The digital citizen is the digital consumer who is increasingly demanding and finds their government lacking. Governments are not agile enough. They need to have adaptive frameworks of laws and legislation; changes in infrastructure are too slow.

A great example is the legislation around drones. Drones have been around for a while, yet in some countries legislation has been tabled but not yet voted on. The governments are so slow and the evolution of technology so fast that there's a clash, a disruption. On privacy issues, healthcare, wearables, face recognition, the governments need to move faster. We need agile governance with frameworks of discovery, so policy makers can find out what consumption is happening, how people are adopting technology and how laws and infrastructure need to change.

Most laws and governments are still country-based. With globalisation there are no digital frontiers. We might argue that Europe, for example, has challenges on physical frontiers, but individuals are borderless in the digital world. And of course there is no national security without cyber-security.

In some countries, companies like Uber are being pursued like today's heretics by government policy makers and the taxi industry. Governments are being challenged to deal with the twenty-four hour always-on economy and allow night work employment. What should a government do, regulate more or de-regulate? What do we want? Unfortunately, history has shown that a higher degree of regulation fosters inertia, and our current laws are not written with digital in mind. Do they defend outdated IP and regulatory legal frameworks or evolve faster to better meet the needs of their citizens and businesses?

The government also has to take care of the non-tech part of the population, the digital ignorants. How do governments around the world reply to the increasing demand of the younger population for service and speed of innovation they get from businesses while coping with the needs of the ageing not-so-tech population? They have to remember there's still a vast number of people not updating their taxes on the web. The question that needs to be answered is how public administration can innovate and modernise its structures, regulations, services and roles to become an agile, responsive and transparent iGov or eGov and help to bridge the digital divide.

And governments need to consider this question at all levels: government to governments (G2G), government to citizens (G2C), government to employees (G2E), government to businesses (G2B) and government to technology (G2T).

The digital enterprise

The digital revolution has created three variations of enterprise:

1 **Digital native enterprises** – the Ubers, Airbnbs, technology and biotech start-ups and organisations. They start with digital as their oxygen. The whole business is run around digital and software is their platform for scale. They use the power of the Cloud, of connection, globalisation, big data; everything is in there. Most often they are in the healthy quadrant on our Dualarity model

2 **Digital incumbents** are crawling but not yet walking in the digital world. They might link themselves with start-ups and try to get involved in the start-up world and mindset, building a strong kernel surrounded with layers of flexibility and fluidity. These companies are really captivating; they're incumbents that do some digital, moving from offline to the online world. They are hiring new talent and re-training their teams. They are in a phase of change, figuring how to do it best. They are mature businesses, but need to become healthy again by adopting digital as their oxygen

3 **Digital immigrants** are struggling to understand. They do not realise that they can put a service and a product together and define innovative features. Most often these enterprises are scared or injured; they may die or they'll be purchased. They can still move to become healthy, because transformation has become the new standard.

Organisations need to ask themselves whether they are disruptive innovators or are they going to be disrupted? Are they in the middle? Are they trying to embrace some pieces of disruption, but not everything? Or do they embrace disruption fully? Are they strong enough to survive a small or large disruptive earthquake? Can they ride the wave of change?

The how-to part will be covered in the 'Energising' section. The Cracking the Dualarity Code part will give insights on how to coach people and businesses sitting in the different quadrants.

Digital Human Side-effects

> We can easily forgive a child who is afraid of the dark; the real tragedy of life is when men are afraid of the light.
>
> Plato

One of the notable issues with the digital revolution is that fear tends to dominate. Some people are finding themselves and their organisations in the scared quadrant as they don't see the opportunities or they focus on the things that go wrong and are risky. How people react in uncertain moments is a good indicator of how they will react in the future. People want transparency and traceability. They want what they lost in the past, that which gave them certainty. The predictive sequence of life, which was learn (start), earn (middle) and return (end), is fundamentally changing, and this puts people in an uncomfortable position. The older people are, the more likely it is they are trying to hold on to this sequence.

Every generation is looking at global warming issues, we have economic challenges, wars, refugees, terrorism and privacy concerns. Even the new Tesla car is ready for biological weapon assaults; by closing all the filters you would be able to survive in it for twenty-four hours.

We hear about changes for the worse in the three things that most people have come to take for granted in past centuries: the church, banks and politics. The church was always there for peace of mind, banks were there to take care of our savings and make our money work, and politics represented us, speaking for the people and ensuring democracy. Most people trusted those three pillars of society.

But now we've lost faith in the church and religion, with the acceleration of extremism, acknowledgement of paedophilia in the Catholic Church and the diminishing numbers believing in a god. We can no longer bank on the banks and financial institutions blindly; they've been going bankrupt, there were scandals, they're not too big to fall, as we saw during the financial crises of 2008, and trust in politicians is at an all-time low. Governments are falling, left and right wings are fighting open battles in the US and clashing in other parts of the world, and fear is being fed by the politicians.

Economic and political instability play a big role in the fear for the future, from Greece and Eastern Europe to Syria, North Africa and North Korea.[102] Then we add technology on top, and many are getting scared for the future of their kids, or worrying about job security and paying for education, healthcare and the cost of living in general. But other countries look very promising, such as India, Indonesia, Mexico, Uruguay, and in Europe where Germany is still going strong, and others like Italy and Spain are on the path of recovery.

Tintin Snack: same, but different. When my son had his twenty-first birthday in 2016 he received a very smart letter from the biggest local newspaper, *Het Laatste Nieuws* (*The Latest News*). It had sent him a printout of its front page from the day he was born. The headlines talked about the bomb assault on Oklahoma, the bankruptcy of Sabena, Belgian's largest aviation group, that had failed as it didn't transfer faster into a modern aviation company, and youngsters being aggrieved at school. Sounds familiar? The funny part is that every generation thinks that the next generation is doomed, but so far they all have been wrong. I believe that humans, society, will continue to exhibit an amazing ability to course correct when the need is there.

So is it the Internet of Things, the Internet of Everything or the Internet of Nothing? Fear and uncertainties too often give people an alibi to postpone decisions or not to act. We should give people the insights and tools to fight fear and transform it into positive energy of change.

Here are some of the side effects of digital adoption being seen right now.

Digital Smombies. If you observe any group of people waiting for a bus, you will see them staring at hand-held devices that transport them to a place that seems so fascinating and acts as their entrance to another world of the digital. We now have smombies, smartphone zombies who are so interested in looking at their phones they don't look up when walking. In Germany – Cologne and Munich – and in the Chinese city Chongqing, there are special smombie lanes to reduce accidents, with the right information painted on the ground so the smombies don't need to look up when crossing the street.

We have people complaining of **infotoxication**. We are exposed to around 3,000 brands per day, and this is increasing through the power of social media. People are going on self-imposed digitoxes, reducing their usage of digital technology.

Digital memory loss. Some side effects of the always-on world is what Scottish researchers diagnosed as the Busy Lifestyle Syndrome.[103] We don't remember less; instead we have too much going on so we can't store it all. Therefore, we compensate by storing information externally. A smartphone is a great tool for doing this, but it's also the reason for the memory loss. A recent study by cybersecurity company Kaspersky Lab[104] talks about 'digital amnesia' where people forget information once it is stored in their digital device. Dr Maria Wimber of Birmingham University mentions that it is easy to store information so we can forget selectively and it frees-up space in our brain, which in a sense is healthy for our brains.

Nomophobia. Today, the smartphone is the extension of human life, almost like a friend. When we ask people to share their phones with each other, we find great resistance, and fear. People don't want to give their phones up for fear of not being connected, which is called nomophobia. If people lose Wi-Fi connection or go to an area of low mobile signal, they often become anxious. Their phone has even become a social partner: when they go to an event and don't know anyone, they look at their phone, their buddy, and then they don't feel isolated.

The digital running thief. Apps like Runkeeper, Nike+ Running, Myrun and Runtastic help you to plan running and biking sprints and keep track of your history. But many runners are, in the spirit of the sharing economy, posting pictures of their expensive bikes and other valuable information, and thieves thrive on digital. If a thief tracks the sports patterns in the app, they even know when the user is away. This can easily be fixed by thinking before posting and by setting the right privacy settings.

The 'Like' culture. The same brain circuits that are activated by eating chocolate and winning money are activated when youngsters see large numbers of 'likes' on their own photos or the photos of peers in a social network, according to a first-of-its-kind UCLA study that scanned teens' brains while they were using social media.[105]

Dualarity of choice. With this digital overload we end up with the paradox of choice. People think that the more choice they have, the easier it is to make a decision. It's just the opposite. When people have too many choices, they are overloaded with too much information. They might not make the right decision, just postpone it or make bad choices. They don't have the courage or energy any more to make a decision; they are injured. The big brands need to figure out that they have too many places on their shelves, too much exposure.

Consumers are getting overloaded by an average of 3,000 commercial brand touches[106] a day, but most don't get noticed. Stores offer between 3,000 and 10,000 items, and on average twenty-two get purchased during a shopping visit. Often the number of items purchased is just one. When consumers say they want more choice, they really mean better choice and a better choosing experience. And too much digital advertising is adding another layer to this overload.

Another problem with infotoxication is it gives people the impression that they have to buy more, they have to consume more.

Apple offers only a limited number of iPhone and iPad models, all with consistent design and branding wherever they are sold, making it easier for people to select. Offline retailers like Tesco and Walmart around the world are acknowledging this challenge and reducing their offerings, while online retailers like Amazon and Bol.com are extending their offering but with an improved choosing experience. More is less.

Changing Customer Journey

> All we have to decide is what to do with the time that is given us.
>
> J.R.R. Tolkien

There is a battle for human attention. There are only twenty-four hours in a day, and we can't buy time. There's only a finite amount of time we can spend on the infinite amount of devices, apps and information sources that are available. Enterprises and individuals need to define why they should put their attention to any one thing. Everyone needs to decide where to spend their human attention.

Whatever artificial intelligence or smart system can help you free time will give you time to pay more attention to things that matter more or most to you. Some people are overburdened; our brains are getting overheated because there's too much information to absorb. The on-demand Millennials want to be in the know; they have fear of missing out (FOMO). Knowing means power, or gives a false feeling of power. People want to be liked, they want to share stuff, and they want to see what others say about them.

On Facebook, we're becoming our own best brand managers. We are smart brand managers because we know when we post a certain type of picture, with a little bit of text and some music, our likes go through the roof. We know exactly what people like to see, what they want to hear.

Technology has changed the whole marketing cycle and automation has become the essential foundation of the customer journey. There used to be a sequential process for selling a product where marketing was very simple: build awareness, people considered the product, then they expressed a preference and made a choice, took action and bought, and when they were satisfied, they were loyal. Today people are open to possibility; they will change their mind multiple times on the way to buying a product.

While in a shop, a potential consumer might check the pricing of the same item in another shop or online. If they're looking to buy a house in one area, they might get a recommendation from a friend or online about a house in a completely different part of the city. They are open to possibility; they're open to change; they will investigate; they will receive multiple inputs at different times. There is no sequence any more. The challenge for every marketing and brand professional is not only to define personas in customer journeys, but to be there at the right moment, at the right time, in the right context.

These personas can be defined by what the consumers do, where they do it and how they do it. If you know that people go on Facebook for certain things, you need to make sure your business is there, in the right place, when the consumer is there – the content in the right context at the right moment. With the changes in big data, always-on technology and the on-demand generation, we can be more sophisticated. If we are looking to sell to business travellers, we can see if they like to take the train or prefer to travel at certain times of the day. The data is there and everything is connected. We can make sure that the customer journey is fluent.

We're seeing a shift in strategy from mainly reactive to a proactive approach in defining customer journeys, and customers will stay because they benefit from the journey itself. Just enhancing a few journeys is tactical; shifting the culture, the mindset and operations to a journey-centric approach is truly strategic and transformational.

Of course, our customers don't want us to become obsessed with them. We can be obsessed about our customer experience, our product and journey, but not the customers. Our customers want to be surprised, do something extra. If we show too much obsession, people get scared, but if we give something extra without being obsessed, that's where we can hit them with a surprise factor.

Changing Role Of Advertising And Its CMO

> Great marketing is about leveraging customer data to
> deliver random acts of kindness surrounding your brand.
>
> **Matt Fleckstein, VP of Marketing Automation at Salesforce**

When thinking about digital transformation and the Fourth
Industrial Revolution, everyone is talking about hiring the right
technology people – the CIOs and CTOs. One role that is often
overlooked is the marketing role. The paradigm has changed
significantly – marketing people are talking directly to the heart of
the business – the customers.

Let's look at how the role of marketing is changing and how
important it is to your business success going forward in the
Dualarity.

The combination of new technologies and innovations in the retail
sector have changed consumer behaviours and habits
fundamentally. Social remains a rock star, video is exploding, mobile
is still the dominating traffic driver, and things like virtual reality
open new doors to creative storytelling and engagement with
brands. All of this is now supported by precision advertising
analytics, hyper-targeting, programmatic audience-buying tools
and huge addictions to social apps and consumption. Add to this
the key drivers of consumer trends that we discussed in the earlier
section of the book and we'll understand things are changing.

Marketing will be context aware, as content without context has
no value. Technologies such as mobile services, beacons, geo-
fencing, push notifications and the IoT will have location and
context rules. Share when it matters most. On top of that, machine
learning will make the organisation smarter as it will learn and

predict behaviours, sense emotions, recognise faces and translate information. The future is about context personalised content giving experiences based on emotions and behaviours.

The Facebooks and Googles of this world know every step we are taking, what we are doing and when. They can almost micro target us to influence our purchasing behaviour. New generations are born with the notion that we can order before midnight and the package will arrive in the next hour. The Generation Z consumers won't wait around to find out if your brand is interesting; they will give you eight seconds to prove it, then they'll move on to something more useful to them. Thirty second adverts won't cut it; you need to be fast and fascinating to make an impact on the Millennials. Marketeers will need to be a master in telling stories in their advertising to capture their attention.

Marketing people will need to organise themselves further around customer experiences, audiences, tribes and less around the classical digital channels such as social, email or search. Many companies are still structured based on the old hierarchies, but it is the customer journey, how they experience that journey, their interests and your product that take centre stage. Authenticity, empathy, connection, surprise and engagement will be predominant when creating content, with technology acting as the glue between them.

If data is the currency of the internet, then the audience is the currency of advertising, and insight is what makes the difference between big data and valuable data. Data insights and audiences are the oil of the healthy marketer. S/he has to become a true Dualarity hero – a healthy marketer living in digital and a commercial master.

Tintin Snack: a Scandinavian media group becoming a data and technology company. In June 2016 I attended WebTomorrow, one of the largest digital events of the year, in Ghent, Belgium. I watched Frederik Karén, Chief Editor of the Swedish newspaper *Svenska Dagbladet Schibsted* media group present in one of the keynotes. Beyond being Editor in Chief, he also covers the commercial and digital strategy.

The media group transformed itself into a tech and data driven media company by hiring 250 developers. It basically took on Google and Facebook Instant Articles head to head by building a platform for content and advertising, with real-time analytics to rate posted content. It tested fremium monetisation models with the twenty-five first articles being free and increased its video coverage.

Karén is convinced that in order to succeed, we need to own our data and technology. The media group addressed big data for precisely targeting its readers and used smart algorithms to automate the order of the news on its website, lowering the cost of producing content while keeping the quality high. Results: besides 120,000 newspaper subscribers, the group added 70% more digital subscribers to reach 25,000. A great story of digital leadership, transformation, reinvention, hiring the right talent and putting the readers at the heart of the company.

Moving forward, Frederik Karén believes the media world will need to collaborate and consolidate internationally to thrive against the Facebooks and Googles of the world.

At the end of the day, it is all about leadership to create the right conditions:

- Understand the customer journey, audiences, tribes, the product or service experiences and the power of data analytics, insights and algorithms.
- Form Industry partnerships. Like consumers don't live inside industry silos. You're competing against everyone
- Have the mindset of the Millennials and digital natives. A fluid organisation can break fixed mindsets
- Build a future-proof organisation with the right skills and increase cross-group collaboration. Roles like CMO, CTO, CDO and CIO need to act as one team, and in some cases become one, being commercial to monetise content and data real-time while connecting with their customers
- Find a good balance between the three connected ingredients of digital transformation: customer at the heart, people as the soul and digital as the oxygen of the company, all aligned to the overarching why and what
- Inspire and be a great storyteller and seller. And yes, be tech savvy enough to lead by example and with authenticity
- See things others don't see (consumer, digital, social-economic) and how to energise your way forward in the future. Trend watching and putting the information at work is the way to go to stay ahead.

My Privacy, My Security

We need to agree that humans are not fail-proof. And by agreeing to this, we assume computers, built by humans, aren't either.

The global power of digital data is very much concentrated around the big tech companies such as Facebook, Google, Apple, Amazon, Microsoft, and Alibaba. As of now Google knows what we are looking for, Amazon and Alibaba know what we are buying and what we like, Apple knows where we are, Facebook knows what we are doing, what we like, saying and who our friends are, and Microsoft knows where we are working. And Chinese companies like Tencent and Wechat are joining this party of being in the know. They all have access to almost unlimited cash and will continue to buy smaller companies to grow their place in the digital marketplace. Microsoft bought LinkedIn and Skype, Instagram and WhatsApp were bought by Facebook, YouTube by Google. And who is next: Twitter, Snapchat?

And the world is reacting. The Austrian privacy activist Max Schrems initiated a lawsuit against the data transfer of Facebook to the US, Europe closed a framing agreement that should regulate data transfer between the US and Europe, and Facebook, YouTube, Twitter, Google and Microsoft have signed the European Union pact, an online 'code of conduct' aimed at fighting hate speech so social media companies can take quick action as soon as a valid notification is received.

The British inventor of the World Wide Web Tim Berners-Lee warned that the freedom of the internet is under threat by governments and corporations interested in controlling the web, as has been shown by the revelation of mass government monitoring of online activities following the leaks by former US intelligence contractor Edward Snowden.

I think the following summarises the challenge at hand very well:

> While the evolution of Cloud computing has transformed the way we work, recent geopolitical events have precipitated debates on the roles that governments and industry should play in defending and securing society, and the appropriate balance between security, privacy and the freedom of expression.
>
> **Brad Smith, President and Chief Legal Officer at Microsoft Corporation**

We need internet that is governed by good law striking the right balance. Government and the industry would need to agree on a digital security framework that determines basic digital rights, obligations and our freedoms. All of them based on the principle of being transparent how data is being used.

As data explodes, data security concerns will explode, as we have seen with the hacking of LinkedIn[107] (117 million), eBay (145 million) and My Space (164 million) accounts. Where it used to be an IT driven discussion, this has now become part of a boardroom discussion in businesses, government and at home as the boundary of the digital work-life has fade.

Tintin Snack: youngsters, despite their digital savviness, are very concerned about their privacy. I was presenting to an audience of 150 marketing students and fifty small and medium businesses (SMBs) on The Age of Transformation as part of a half day programme on the future of advertising and the impact of digital. During the Q&A, privacy and security were addressed and it was an animated debate. To my surprise, it was not the SMBs who had a lot of questions, it was the students who were very vocal. This confirms what some studies show about Millennials being concerned about privacy.

The tech industry, and in particular the big tech giants, has a crucial role in the discussion on privacy with the abundance of data at its disposal. The industry's role as a moral compass increases and deep introspection is an essential part of protecting our digital lives – finding the right balance between personal privacy, freedom of expression and public safety. A balance between respect for national sovereignty and global open markets.

And we as a society play a huge role in educating our children in digital skills like safety, security and identity management.

We need a three-way play between government, the industry and society to find the Dualarity between privacy and freedom where we need to agree that a zero risk society will not exist.

The Future Of Work Dualarity

Every great work of art has two faces, one toward its own time and one toward the future, toward eternity.

Lester Bangs, The Smart Automated World Creating Challenges And Opportunities

How we define the future timescale will give different answers to the pressing question of the future of work. We can read the different research articles, but most predictions only go up to 2025. Very few have tried to model the future of work beyond that point. The Black Swan theory, popularised by Nassim Nicholas Taleb, is a metaphor that describes a surprise event that has a major effect, and is then inappropriately rationalised after the fact with the benefit of hindsight. It is very hard to predict the future as we don't know what we don't know. But future thinking is about thinking ahead: thinking about what we can see today so we can make the world a better place and take the right actions to steer it in the right direction. A future that is worth wanting.

Moving forward towards an intelligent, more automated workforce will not just replace jobs but will transform jobs as we know them today. Parts of the job will get automated, jobs will disappear and new jobs will see the light of day. This is nothing new as innovations and automation of the workforce have been taking place during the past few industrial revolutions in the 19th and 20th centuries. Many manufacturing jobs have been replaced by automation, and so many more jobs will change as computers become more intelligent. We call them robots, our children and grandchildren might call them colleagues.

Historically, technological innovation in previous revolutions has produced growing incomes and higher standards of living for many. Will this be the case with the digital revolution? A difference with the digital revolution is the speed at which it is happening, although it still might take decades before we see the full impact. Innovations are transforming companies, industries, government, society and us as individuals. Some people, parts and geographies will find it easy to adapt, while others will be challenged by the implications of the digital revolution on the future of work, our way of living, standards of life, the equality gap and physical mobility.

As in every economic development, people tend to move towards the cities when a country reaches a certain level of technological adoption. In Africa there will be a huge change as people will cluster around cities. They'll need electricity first, as there are still 1.3 billion people with no access to something that basic. Then they'll install the internet – 4 billion have no access to internet today – and migrate towards cities and other countries. This will impact existing jobs in many industries, create new jobs and have huge implications in different geographies around the world.

Let us take a peek at a few interesting research studies on the future of work.

A 2016 PWC study[108] on the status of the digital business within companies across twenty-six developed countries showed that 33% have achieved advanced levels of digitisation and 72% will have reached that stage by 2020. Investments in the Industrial Revolution 4.0 are expected to cost around 5% of the annual revenues, with 50% of companies expecting a return of investment (ROI) within two years, reducing cost by 3.6% per year and increasing efficiency by 4.1%. All this will be fuelled by data science and analytics driving the majority of future decision-making, while cybersecurity will remain the number one concern. The big benefits will demand a true digital culture and investment in re-skilling or attracting new capabilities such as data scientists and algorithmists. While Japan and Germany focus more on efficiency and product quality, the US is far more focused on new digital business models and services, hence the boom of innovation, business disruptors and start-ups.

> If you don't have a real stake in the new, then just surviving on the old – even if it is about efficiency – I don't think is a long-term game.
>
> **CEO Microsoft, Satya Nadella**

Let us now take a closer look at three recent Future of Work studies from the Oxford Martin School.

A 2013[109] study called 'The Future of Employment: How susceptible are jobs to computerisation?' from Oxford professors Carl Frey and Michael Osbourne looked into the jobs that would be vulnerable to computerisation from AI and robotics. Their model predicts that up to 47% of US jobs in 2010 are highly likely to become computerised in the next ten to twenty years, and transportation, logistics and administrative occupations would be the most vulnerable. Jobs that are at risk are drivers, travel agents, tax advisors, receptionists, assistants; those less at risk are the jobs that require more creativity and social intelligence such as healthcare and education. They will be mainly human-driven, even if some sub tasks might get automated.

A 2015 research study from the University of Oxford and Citi[110] 'Technology at Work Citi GPS Report' showed that 85% of jobs, mostly in developing economies, might be at risk – 69% in India and 77% in China. Some of these countries are referred to as the fabric of the world, and with technologies like robots, AI and 3D printing, the manufacturing industry could take place closer to the consumption with more automation in manufacturing plants. Advances in 3D printing in manufacturing could potentially impact more than 320 million manufacturing jobs. It will be critical when this happens that these people get re-skilled ready for the future world, and that developed countries unite and unify policies and strategies to enable them to migrate, at the same time solving some of the ageing challenges in developed countries. If that doesn't happen we will risk increased inequality and an ageing population in developed countries posing a challenge for the economic prosperity, in need of younger demographics. Developed and developing countries need each other to thrive in this Fourth Industrial Revolution, a dualarity.

A third publication from the same authors was released in 2016. Called 'Technology At Work v 2.0: The future is not what it used to be', it builds on the first two reports mentioned above:

In addition to providing remarkable achievements in technology, the digital age has also decreased labour's share of GDP. The digital age has benefited consumers, and shareholders, but not necessarily workers.

J.P. Gownder, a Boston-based technology research analyst from Forrester, takes a more conservative view. He predicts that automation will create a net loss of only 9.1 million US jobs by 2025. The horizon of his study is much closer, but his numbers are well under the roughly 70 million jobs that Frey and Osbourne from the Oxford Martin School believe to be in danger of vaporisation. He says, 'In reality, automation will spur the growth of many new jobs – including some entirely new job categories.'

Derek Thomson, an editor at *The Atlantic*, summarises the arguments for why automation will replace labour permanently in 'A World Without Work'.[111] The Bank of England has issued a warning that in the UK alone some 15 million jobs are at risk over the next twenty years.

> The Fourth Industrial Revolution, combined with other socio-economic and demographic changes, will transform labor markets in the next five years, leading to a net loss of over 5 million jobs in 15 major developed and emerging economies. The global workforce is expected to experience significant churn between job, families and functions over the period 2015–2020, with a total loss of 7.1 million jobs – two thirds of which are concentrated in routine white collar office functions, such as office and administrative roles – and a total gain of 2 million jobs, in computer and mathematical and architecture and engineering related fields.

> **World Economic Forum[112] (WEF) 2015**

And in China we see dark factories[113] popping up as robots take over. Completely automated, they operate in the dark with no human interaction. One example of a changing city in China is Dongguan where 43,684 workers were replaced with robots in 2015, cutting costs at the factories by nearly 10%.

Seeing the opportunities of robots and jobs

You can check what CEO and founder of i4j David Nordfors, who works with Vint Cerf, an American Internet pioneer recognized as one of the fathers of the Internet, has to say in his article[114] 'Is Unemployment A Problem Or An Opportunity? How Much Value Can You Create If You Hate Or Are Indifferent To Your Job? And What Changes If You Are Actually Passionate About It?' Or read the forward thinking of Modis in 'Tech jobs On the Rise'[115] who predicts an increase of 658,000 jobs in the US by 2020 driven by growth in health, IT, data analysis, programming and SW engineering, DB development and business intelligence, security and web development. Healthcare could have a massive shortage of qualified workers, 13 million, by 2035.

Martin Ford, author of the *Financial Times* awarded book *The Rise Of The Robots: Technology and the threat of a jobless future,* sees a future where no one should perform a job that is boring, repetitive or dangerous.

Arie Van Den Eynde, Director of the research facility Robovalley in Delft, Netherlands, says that we should not fear robots, and Pieter Abbeel, Professor at Berkeley Artificial Research Laboratory in California and researcher of OpenAI, is working on a robot[116] for ironing to help families with one of the most repetitive and time consuming tasks. So robots will help us to extinguish all boring and repetitive tasks at home, making our life easier.[117]

Life is very full and every minute overflowing with possibility!
Max McKeown

What type of jobs will be hot or not?

The well-known sociologist Manuel Castells divided jobs into generic routine jobs, such as receptionists, accountants, administrators, which are at high risk, and self-programmable jobs requiring cognitive tasks like creativity and emotional intelligence, such as therapists and teachers, which are at a lower risk. Everyone will require life-long learning to cope with the changes inherent in the digital revolution.

McKinsey's report of November 2015 added a view that only some parts of jobs might get automated, making jobs more appealing and meaningful. A 2016 Australian report from the Commonwealth Scientific and Industrial Research Organization, CSIRO[118], looked at the workplace megatrends for Australia over the next twenty years. By 2035 we will see the birth of newly created human-only driven jobs such as:

- Remote pilots to control future unmanned vehicles
- Online chaperones to provide support for online activity, from protection from fraud and identity theft to social media and reputation management
- Personalised preventative health helpers with great people skills and the ability to interpret and understand health and wellbeing data. As populations are ageing and living – wanting to live – longer, the demand for these roles will increase substantially
- The need for big data analysts will continue to expand rapidly, along with specialisation of analyst roles.

Researchers at Oxford University compiled a study that looked at nine variables for more than 700 job descriptions, predicting how likely it is that a computer could take over the job[119] and assessing which jobs will remain in the human only spectrum.

Function	Probability of Automation (%)
Telemarketers	99
Loan Officers	98
Receptionists and Information Clerks	96
Paralegals and Legal Assistants	94
Budget analysts	94
Retail Salespersons	92
Taxi Drivers and Chauffeurs	89
Security Guards	84
Cooks, Fast Food	81
Bartenders	77
Computer Support Specialist	65
Personal Financial Advisors	58
Advertising Sales Agent	54
Computer Programmers	48
Reporters and Correspondents	11
Musicians and Singers	7.4
Writers and Authors	3.8
Computer and Information System Manager	3.5
Lawyers	3.5
Chiropractors	2.7
Art Directors	2.3
Marketing Managers	1.4
Sales Managers	1.3
Nurses	0.9
Elementary School Teachers	0.4
Physicians and Surgeons	0.4

Sources University of Oxford, Carl Benedikt Frey
and Michael A. Osborne 2013

Futurist Thomas Frey predicts, '60% of the best jobs in the next 10 years haven't been invented yet'. Remember, in the past careers were built on the learn-earn-return sequence of life. We used to have long careers, mostly loyal to a few companies, where today there are multiple mini-careers as fixed term employees or freelancers. Some examples of the most likely in-demand careers in the next ten years, as published by Sparks & Honey, are: productivity counsellors, personal digital curator, corporate disorganiser (an expert shuffling hierarchies in companies to create a start-up culture or organised chaos), 3D–4D printing handyman, digital detox therapist, crowdsourcing specialist, privacy counsellor, drone drivers and urban shepherd.

In the short term, more people will want flexi-jobs and to work in flexible co-working spaces spread around the country so they can avoid traffic, solving some of the mobility issues. They will become islands of creativity, people meeting at different locations to work. These business nomads will only need the internet, a laptop, a coffee and a cosy environment to be creative. The tribal workforce gets the flexibility of work and the employer is spreading the start-up mentality, keeping and attracting the younger generations.

In summary, whatever happens, whatever datapoints you believe or want to believe, we will need new skills, cultures and mindsets to make the most of the digital revolution. This will demand cross border collaboration of governments, companies, education, scientists and every person on this planet. Both developed countries and developing countries will have their challenges, and we need to put our society and industry to work for us to thrive in the digital age.

Business leaders will need to define what skills they want to bring in, and what skills need to be developed to create a competitive advantage. Parents will need to assess what is best for their children and what type of education is needed. Professionals will need to determine if they are on a hot seat or need to learn new skills. For all of these, constant learning will become the new norm.

> Instead of wringing our hands and blaming technology, we should be rolling up our sleeves to ensure that people who lose their jobs to technology are being retrained. This also requires patience – recognizing that it will take time for these workers to be re-employed in higher-skilled jobs.[120]

Starting up

Why are start-up shooting up like mushrooms around the world? Why are there so many of them, all with their own ecosystems? Some people say they create a start-up because they love the freedom to create, to be innovative, or they want to have impact, adventure and variety. Others do it to become the next Facebook, or the next unicorn business (any non-public trading tech start-up company that reaches a $1billion market value). All start-ups believe their baby is the best and most beautiful. And even if it's a very ugly baby, everyone says it's beautiful.

Entrepreneurship is hot because everybody wants a part of it – the investors, the business angels, financers, accelerators, coaches, mentors, tech gurus, experts, workshops, boot camps, juries, awards, competitions and the incumbents. The ecosystem is massive. There are cool working spaces, and every company wants a shiny start-up garage. Existing companies are making their own garage environments where they will host five or six start-ups. Others are setting up cocktail bars to attract people. Many tactics are at hand that will need to be complemented with deeper change.

You can survive in this ecosystem for a long time. Entrepreneurship is hot and youngsters are attracted by it. But if you look at the trajectory of start-ups, after the initial thrills of the start-up summit, boot camp, making the plan, building your team, investor pitches, etc. comes the growth stage. The growth stage is where the most skeletons are found.

> **Tintin Snack: from hero to zero.** But not all is rosy. More than 90% of start-ups fail before they start scaling. And others fail because they've oversold themselves or haven't followed the rules. The thirty-

two-year-old start-up wonder Elisabeth Holmes, founder of start-up Theranos, who created new innovative ways of doing virus blood testing through a simple finger prick, went from hero to zero in one year. One of the most disruptive stories in Silicon Valley, they were originally valued at $9 billion and ranked at the top of the richest self-made women. Forbes calculated she was worth $4.5 billion until *Wall Street Journal* discovered that her technology was not what it was made out to be and her testing methods were not following the rules. She was banned from running a laboratory for two years in 2016 and her billions evaporated.

The Educational Rollercoaster Or Reset

Schools, universities and the academic world will act as trees, generating the oxygen of the digital revolution by developing skills and capabilities to future-proof and make learners ready for the 21st century. The distance between the skills needed for the jobs of yesterday and the ones of tomorrow is widening. Fundamentally education has not truly evolved over the past few decades, and an educational digital evolution is not defined by using iPads in the classroom or one or two hours of IT classes.

> **Tintin Snack: teaching didn't change.** In 2014 my son decided to start his five year studies of Business Engineering at the University of Ghent, the same studies as I completed at Brussels University 1988–1992. What had changed since then? The presentations are done in PowerPoint with video and a student university website. Beyond that nothing had changed in more than twenty-five years. It was as if time hadn't moved on, despite the digital revolution, having digital at our fingertips, the new digital savvy generations, the entrepreneur and start-up culture.

How do we adapt the current models of education to bring it closer to the real world? How do we save students from boredom? How do we teach in an appealing way? How do we integrate business with students? How do we give the same access to the poorest and the richest in our society? How do we leverage the newest innovations like artificial intelligence, bots, virtual reality, 3D printing and gamification in the classroom?

AI could help us, through machine learning, to personalise education as it could learn from each student. Gamification could be used to reward and motivate people. Remote access to educational platforms, like the Peer-to-Peer University, Khan Academy, Coursera, etc., already give us a whole offering of online educational courses. The MOOCs (Massive Open Online Courses) allow educators to create courses and reach students wherever they are in the world. Are we going to see an educational world that's future-proof, flexible and adjusted to the needs of today and tomorrow? This debate is heating up around the world.

The question is how do we not only teach the basics, but also prepare students for tomorrow's job market where innovation will automate some tasks or replace jobs? Completely new jobs are being created and specialised skills are needed to cope with the robots and sensors of the future. Teachers and the education system need to embrace the mindset of the digital future by seeing what is happening and understanding new generations.

'Schools and universities should not be built to produce more teachers and professors,' Sir Ken Robinson, English author, speaker and international advisor on education in the arts to the government, non-profits, education and arts bodies, once said, 'but should help them to unleash their creativity, and focus on how to be creative with technology.'

This race for talent is happening in all parts of the world, across all industries, sectors and establishments. We will need an education system that people can go to for constant learning at different stages of their lives. In the old sequence of learn, earn and return, the main constant will be learning. If we don't sign up, we risk being left behind. The way we think about constantly enhancing our teams' capability and technology adoption, as well as spurring creativity, is already a critical differentiator. As Albert Einstein said, 'Imagination is more important than knowledge.'

How can we try to address this? A second language is a must have for new generations. That second language should be computer coding. Teaching people to code opens them up to the digital world. There are many initiatives, like CoderDojo and Minecraft for schools, around the globe to help get more people coding, and attract more women and get youngsters exposed to it faster. Digital seeing is the language of understanding in this new digital world. Programming teaches us how to think logically and how to solve problems going far beyond the one or two hour IT courses we know today.

The language of understanding is digital seeing.

The World Economic Forum published the 'Eight Digital Skills We Must Teach Our Children'.[121] Those skills, called Digital Intelligence or DQ, are a set of social, emotional and cognitive abilities to make children ready for their digital life, covering areas like safety, digital identity and digital communication, and they're all embedded in core values and norms such as respect, empathy and prudence. Governments, schools and parents will need to work hand-in-hand to make these skills happen as they will need new types of teachers, and teachers to teach teachers.

There are also people coding DNA, just like they develop code for programs. Some industries are trying to put data into DNA, not just decrypting the DNA but defining how DNA functions.

In addition to coding skills, only 18% of companies believe they have the skills necessary to gather and use insights effectively. Only 19% of companies are confident that their insight-gathering processes contribute directly to sales effectiveness.[122] Simply collecting data does not unleash its business effectiveness. It's not the amount of data that's important, it's what we do with the data that matters. We need the talent to understand, organise and report on the data so we can use it. These data skills need to be taught.

In her book *Rookie Smarts: Why learning beats knowing in the new game of work*, leadership expert Liz Wiseman explains how experience can be a curse. Being in the mature quadrant of the Dualarity model can actually hold you back:

> Careers stall, innovation stops, and strategies grow stale. Being new, naïve, and even clueless can be an asset. For today's knowledge workers, constant learning is more valuable than mastery.

As you can see, new capabilities and skills are needed for the jobs of the future. Digital literacy is needed together with numeracy and literacy. And STEM (Science, Technology, Engineering and Mathematics) will remain important, but will need to evolve. As Peter Vander Auwera, Co-founder of Innotribe: SWIFT's innovation initiative, says, 'Add the A of Art to STEM and you have STEAM. STEAM would also be reformulated as Social, Technologies, Entrepreneurship, Aesthetics and Mindfulness.'

We might see the emergence of the University of Things connected to the Internet of Things and to business.

Move yourself into the healthy quadrant. Be open for constant learning. Remember, complacency is the curse in the mature quadrant.

In the 'Dualarity Toolbox' we will cover how to gamify teaching and be creative with technology.

Basic Human Needs And Guaranteed Incomes

The solution to poverty is to abolish it directly by a now widely discussed measure: the guaranteed income.

Martin Luther King

Tintin Snack: the human basic needs. A Syrian fleeing his country was asked in a TV interview why he was fleeing; why he didn't remain at the borders of Syria and Turkey. He said, 'I first need three things: food, shelter and safety for my family. And I need my kids to get educated, develop and learn.' As well as the basics, love and friendship, to develop and learn, are important. Abraham Maslow in his 1943 paper 'A Theory of Human Motivation' described what has become known as the hierarchy of human needs, in this order: physiological (food, water, shelter, clothing), safety, belongingness and love, esteem, self-actualisation, and self-transcendence. Digital can address and enhance some layers of the pyramid, but it can't replace others. It might help to get us through the first layer faster so that human beings have more time for love, being esteemed and self-transcending.

To meet the basic needs what can society do? There's a life debate going on over the notion of a guaranteed income or universal business income first introduced by free-market economist Milton Friedman after World War II. If we have fewer jobs in the future, what will people do to make money, to make ends meet? If we have a guaranteed income, so income is not related to work only, and we divide the work equally, we'll have more time to do other things, to be creative. We should be able to earn more, but of course we would have to work more. This system would not supplement existing systems but replace all silo systems as we know them today, which could limit the impact on the lower and middle classes of task and job robotisation. Multiple countries are in evaluation, and countries such as the Netherlands and Finland will start a testing phase in 2017. Both employer and employee are seriously evaluating their options on this type of income, asking how it can solve problems facing the future of work and what its implications would be on our society.

In 2015, 193 world leaders committed to the Global Goals for Sustainable Development to achieve three extraordinary things in the next fifteen years: end extreme poverty, fight inequality and injustice and fix climate change. As Sir Ken Robinson says, 'If every school in the world teaches children about these goals, we will help them become the generation that changed the world.' And if we add digital skills to that we will also secure future jobs and success for them.

In the first part of the 20th century, economists predicted that to live, sustain our lives and be happy, we should only work around one third of the time. The rest of the time we'll be going to the opera, listening to music, going to the movies and enjoying travel. Those predictions didn't stand the test of the free market forces as the power of marketing after World War II created needs we didn't have before, and people started working harder to be able to pay for them. As we got exposed to more products, more brands, more choice, it created a need to consume and buy everything in twos like cars, phones, televisions.. Both husband and wife ended up working to cover the consumer needs.

Summary Of Seeing

The only true wisdom is in knowing you know nothing.

Socrates

Today we can solve paradoxes like combining customisation with scale or increasing productivity while becoming more ecologically sustainable. We can thrive in the Dualarity. We have the opportunity to create organisations that take better care of the earth's resources, of customers, of us.

The Fourth Industrial Revolution, with an exponential acceleration of technological advances, will lead to opportunities, and as with every revolution it will pose some important challenges for our economy and society.[123] The relationship between humans and computers will evolve. Klaus Schwab, Founder and Chairman World Economic Forum (WEF), said, 'Industry 4.0 will not only change what we do, but also who we are.'

Our future holds great opportunity but new risks at the same time. Some people will not be sure this is for them. And right now you might find yourself in the camp of the believers or in the camp of the non-believers. Some might feel like they're sitting on a burning platform in the open sea, waiting for the perfect storm to hit. Some might not take action and wait like the boiling frog to be cooked.

Are you scared, injured, healthy or mature?

Today's technology is different than what we've seen in the past. The technology is taking on cognitive tasks. We now have machines and algorithms that can, at least in a limited sense, think.

Martin Ford, the author of the recent book *Rise Of The Robots: Technology and the threat of a jobless future.*

It is impossible to stay neutral as everyone has their opinions about why they might like or not like the future. Different scenarios can come to life where humans rule machines, or where machines rule humans, or most likely, where humans and machines find a way of existing together. Whether you see the glass half empty or half full, or you are just happy to have a glass, will determine how you approach the future.

So how can you make the most of whatever is in your glass?

On one hand, advances in biotech and new material science will help us to solve issues in the energy and health arenas, connect people and enrich lives, finding cures for diseases like cancer that are incurable today by repairing genes or producing 3D printed body parts. This will create new jobs[124] that don't even exist today, and we might be able to come closer to the meaning of life and what truly counts by digitally delegating repetitive tasks to humanoids.

On the other hand, the challenges will be to manage the disappearance of jobs, the move from manufacturing to an automated or service-driven economy, ethics, privacy and control, and bridging the gaps between inequality of wealth, skills, gender and access to innovations. And all of this while we take care of the earth's limited resources.

Whatever happens, we humans will need to prepare mentally for a huge change and determine the relationship we want to have with robots. Can we co-exist and find the right balance? Do we believe that the losses on one side will be compensated by the gains on the other? As with everything, the truth will be somewhere in the middle, and of course humans will play a critical role. Let's stay alert, keep moving forwards, create energy and have the courage to see and to act rather than holding on to the past.

Living in the land of chocolate, Belgium, I agree with Forrest Gump when he says, 'Life is like a box of chocolates, you never know what you are going to get.' I try to see the possibility of the possibility. Join me on the journey to the future that is here already so we can craft a balanced society and industry together, one that is harmonious, healthy and happy. Why not give it a chance? We have many challenges today, and this might bring us on to the next step of humankind.

So where are you? Who are you? Who can you become?

> The pessimist complains about the wind; the optimist expects it to change; the realist adjusts the sails.
>
> **William Arthur Ward**

Are you a healthy optimist, always trying new things with plenty of energy, exploring the magic of what the future will bring? Are you a mature realist, who has wisdom and two feet on the ground? Are you an injured pessimist who has tried to keep moving ahead, but feels confused and lacks energy? Or are you a scared defeatist, who is sure this new digital revolution will bring doom?

When you find the energy to move between healthy and mature, and keep the energy moving, you can become a Dualarist – living in the Dualarity of performing and transforming. A Dualarity hero.

I hope the above has helped you to see the digital future in a different way and given you a broader context on the drivers and possible implications for society, your business and you. Seeing is the starting point; it sets a level for your knowing so you can gain more energy, peace of mind and the ability to take the right actions for you, your family, your friends, your peers and your business. Now you can leverage some of the energising principles and how-tos in the next section, a non-exhaustive list that is the outcome of my soft and hard lessons in life.

> Impossible is just a big word thrown around by small men who find it easier to live in the world they've been given than to explore the power they have to change it. Impossible is not a fact. It's an opinion. Impossible is not a declaration. It's a dare. Impossible is potential. Impossible is temporary. Impossible is nothing.
>
> **Muhammed Ali, the greatest boxer of all times**

Energise Your Way Forward

Energise
Your Way Forward

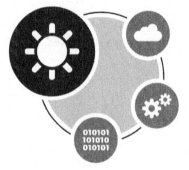

With all of the changes upon us, we have the opportunity to create soulful and highly energised organisations and individuals. This demands different elements to collaborate hand in hand. Absorb energy that gives you light in the dark, warms up the cold, fuels the body and mind and powers your way forward to fly like a butterfly in the digital world, from one flower to another under a blue sky, healthy and mature, away from the scared, away from the injured.

To be able to energise yourself and others, it's important to understand how people reflect and how the brain works.

The brain is the most complex part of a human, but for simplicity reasons let's focus on the two main connected parts. The lower part is the limbic (emotional) system and the higher part, the cortex, is the rational brain. When people hear, see or feel something, they react on the emotional level first. When someone falls over, first they'll feel the pain, then they'll be rational and realise it's only a minor scratch. Both parts of the brain work in balance. If you translate this into the why, what and how of Simon Sinek, the rational part would be the what and the emotional part would be the why and how. So we'll need to shoot for the heart first, then capture minds. This is human behaviour and defines who we are.

The next section will start with the basic principles of the Dualarity and some how-tos to get you energised in your personal and business transformation.

Dualarity Principles

> He who lives in harmony with himself lives in harmony with the universe.
>
> **Marcus Aurelius**

For most of my life I've sought harmony. This quest probably intrigues the vast majority of people looking for answers. What is the meaning of life? What is life? When is life worthy of being lived? How do I find peace of mind?

In the past few years I've gathered some critical life insights – my life principles. As part of my personal transformation, maturing over time (some might call it getting older, and hopefully wiser), moving through the quadrants, changing from scared to healthy again, I have found these principles have helped me to get energised. While these principles alone won't solve the big problems in the world like global warming, terrorism and the plight of millions of refugees, applying some of them will make you more energised to contribute and cope with what you see. Traditional linear thinking is insufficient.

The journey is never complete; it shouldn't end. It is personal and it can mean different things to different people. You will no doubt find other principles. Read through mine, use what works for you, decide which ones you would like to follow.

This section is broken into two Dualarities – 'Transform your personal life' and 'Transform your business life' principles.

Transform Your Personal Life	Transform Your Business Life
✓ Transform Yourself so You can Transform Others, Lead Yourself so you can Lead Others ✓ Be the Master of Your Own Fate ✓ Your Ego should not be Bigger than your Talent ✓ Do Everything With passion ✓ People never Forget how you made them Feel ✓ Envy is Not The Same as Admiration ✓ Don't live Someone else's life ✓ Good relationships build Happy lives ✓ Life is not a Rehearsal ✓ Learn, Un-learn and Re-Learn	✓ Find Harmony in Disharmony ✓ Beyond the Rules ✓ How Older and Incumbent can be Young and Disruptive ✓ Work is Life and Life is Work ✓ Learn to Fail Successfully ✓ You can get what you Expect, without the Need to Inspect ✓ Give room to Newborns

You need to energise yourself before you can energise others. You can't give what you don't have.

Transform your personal life

It's one of the characteristics of a leader that he does not doubt for one moment the capacity of the people he's leading to realize whatever he's dreaming. Imagine if Martin Luther King had said, 'I have a dream. Of course, I'm not sure they'll be up to it.'

Benjamin Zander

Transform yourself so you can transform others, lead yourself so you can lead others. Before you can lead others, you need to know where you are going. Benjamin Zander, English Conductor and Musical Director of the Boston Philharmonic Youth Orchestra, explains eloquently that great leaders are masters in leading everyone to a destination. To lead everyone you need the why – your purpose. The destination has to have a why. For people to follow you, rally around an idea and go forward, they must see the world of possibility. Leaders are our star thinkers; they see the world as full of opportunities. Break the discouraging, scared downward spiral and help people move into the healthy quadrant.

Great leaders make things beautiful so people care.

Tintin Snack: engage everybody by being engaged. As I learned when I was younger, it is easy to fall into the trap when you have an idea of charging forwards, designing the whole project or the idea yourself, and at the 90% mark asking the team to engage with the final 10%. Then it's still your idea. Nobody is connected with your project. If you fail, you fail; if you're successful you're successful.

Over time it became clear to me that we not only need to make things beautiful and make an idea look good, but we need to make the team part of the idea from the start. Instead of going to your team or colleagues with 90% and everything defined, go with 30% and let the team come up with 70% of the project. Then success and failure is for the whole team; everyone will feel accountable as you stand as one group behind the idea, and the crowd will have made your initial idea ten times better.

If your organisation is not transforming fast enough it is probably because you haven't started with your own transformation. It is about understanding who you are, what you want, why you want it. Give a meaning to yourself, so you can give a meaning to your team.

When one changes, others are destined to change as a consequence.

Be the Master of your Fate – be the Captain of your Soul
William Ernest Henley, 1892

Be the master of your own fate. A few years ago I went to South Africa with my family, visiting my sister who lives there. During our stay we visited Nelson Mandela's prison on Robben Island, where he spent eighteen of his twenty-seven years of imprisonment in a room of around 2 square metres. This left a lasting impression on me and my family – admiration for his will to live, to survive, and eventually thrive.

Instead of blaming circumstances, governments, corporations, others or even ourselves, we need to take ownership of our journeys whenever possible. Take responsibility for our future, our actions, our fate.

John Carlin recounts in his book *Playing the Enemy: Nelson Mandela and the Game That Made a Nation* the events in South Africa before and during the 1995 Rugby World Cup, and following the dismantling of apartheid. Mandela claims that the words of the poem 'Invictus' kept him alive during his most difficult years, and later *Invictus* was released as a movie on the big screen. (If you look on YouTube for *Invictus* – Poem That Inspired A Nation, you will understand what I mean.) The epicentre of the poem is the mind, the body and the soul.

Invictus

Out of the night that covers me,
Black as the pit from pole to pole,
I thank whatever gods may be
For my unconquerable soul.
In the fell clutch of circumstance
I have not winced nor cried aloud.
Under the bludgeonings of chance
My head is bloody, but unbowed.
Beyond this place of wrath and tears
Looms but the Horror of the shade,
And yet the menace of the years
Finds and shall find me unafraid.
It matters not how strait the gate,
How charged with punishments the scroll,
I am the master of my fate,
I am the captain of my soul.

William Henley, 1892

Be the captain of your journey as the journey is the reward.

The ego is a fascinating monster.

Alanis Morissette

Your ego shouldn't be bigger than your talent. In *Leading from the Emerging Future: From ego-system to eco-system economies,* Otto Scharmer and Katrin Kaufer advocate that we change from an obsolete 'ego-system' focused entirely on the wellbeing of ourselves to an eco-system that emphasises the wellbeing of the whole. Instead of having a lot of egos competing, create a sharing, collaborative environment. When we remove the egos and ask people to contribute, they can learn from others.

Tintin Snack: let your talent sing. Coldplay are a wonderful example as they use music to tell stories and create beautiful, captivating experiences. The lead singer leaves his ego at the door. The group, the whole is more important. He lets his talent sing as part of the group.

This is the century of we,[125] not the century of I. There is a unity in the Dualarity. When our ego is not larger than our talent and we leave our ego at the door, we are able to help others to learn while helping ourselves.

Passion is the thing that will help you create the highest expression of your talent.

Larry Smith

Do everything with passion. In my opinion, work has to be what makes you tick and gives expression to your passion. You have to invest in life and get a return on those investments, so do everything with passion and follow your heart whenever possible. It is like gardening: nature gives you back what you invest in it. Shoot for the heart and the mind will follow. Share your passion and you'll make others sparkle with you.

Tintin Snack: play with passion. I recall a business event called Leaders in London where the vast majority of the 900 strong executive audience looked grey. With very few exceptions they were wearing grey or black. Then Benjamin Zander came on stage with a piano and a cello. He talked about a few principles of life, the connection between music and business, and then moved on to play music with passion, showing how to make a difference.

He selected a victim, who had the misfortune to have a birthday that day, to come to the stage and stand on the table, and he asked the audience to sing 'Happy Birthday'. Nine hundred apathetic voices mumbled 'Happy Birthday' because Benjamin Zander had asked them to. Zander then taught the group to sing 'Happy Birthday' from the heart, with passion, with energy. Finally, he asked the birthday boy how he felt.

The man replied, 'I was elevated, I felt like I was flying.'

When you do anything with passion, with emotion, with energy, other people feel it. They also feel it when you don't. So play from the heart, put emotion into everything you do. It will make your organisation and yourself more resilient to change.

Passion equals learning, learning equals knowledge, and knowledge equals respect. And this respect needs to be mutual to succeed.

I've learned that people will forget what you said, people will forget what you did, but people will never forget how you made them feel.

Maya Angelou, American poet, storyteller, activist, and autobiographer 1928–2014

People never forget how you made them feel. Think about your neighbours, your family, your friends, past colleagues, even people you haven't seen for years. We always remember people for how they made us feel, not for what they said or did. Whether we're a manager, a partner in a relationship, with our parents or our children, we have to think about what we do and say and how it makes others feel, because that's what makes a connection.

Remember to shoot for the heart, leave your ego at the door, and that people feel before their mind takes action.

> It would be wonderful to enjoy success without seeing envy in the eyes of those around you.
>
> **Marilyn Monroe**

Envy is not the same as admiration. The point when we start to think that people around us are becoming too successful or too smart, and instead of admiring them and working with them, we become envious, is when we fall into the injured quadrant. Jealousy hurts our businesses and ourselves.

Tintin Snack: 'Why People Hate Microsoft and What To Do To Be Loved' lecture of 2003 – Max McKeown. Microsoft were having challenges with the justice departments in the European Union and the US about their position in the market when prolific UK author, Max McKeown, came along in the summer of 2003 to talk to a company meeting of 300 people from the Benelux group on how Microsoft was perceived at that time. On stage, he presented himself as a corporate activist – in worn-out jeans. He was able to connect with the audience and produced a passionate, energising session, helping Microsoft to understand why people hated it at that point and what to do to be loved.

The admiration for golden duo Bill Gates and Microsoft had become envy. When we become *too* successful, people will try to find weaknesses and their feelings shift into envy. Microsoft learned a lot, and with the right actions since then have continued to be one of the most admired brands in the world.

Don't fall into this trap. Learn from others, admire them for who they are, but don't waste time on judging and envying them. When you see others who are healthier, wealthier or more successful than you, look at what you can learn from them.

> The heaviness of being successful was being replaced by the lightness of being a beginner again.
>
> **Stanford University commencement speech by Steve Jobs**

Don't live someone else's life. Life is too short. It might not always be what we expect of it at every moment, but time is the only life ingredient that can't be extended by an app. Use your time on this planet wisely; every minute counts. Live your life with your heart and soul, with energy and passion, and while doing so try to take care of the planet as we only have one. Don't let other people or society determine what you need to do, how you need to live and who you need to be. Always stay true to yourself, and don't sacrifice that for anyone. I love people not for what they do but for who they are.

In his Stanford University commencement speech, Steve Jobs, CEO and co-founder of Apple and Pixar, urges us to pursue our dreams and see the opportunities in life's setbacks – including death itself.

Don't copy other leaders, don't copy other businesses or the Ubers of this world, don't copy Silicon Valley. Instead take the learnings, give them your own flavour and make them your own.

Good relationships build happy lives. A Harvard Study of adult development, the longest study of adult life (seventy-five years!)[126] that's ever been done, showed that good relationships keep us happier and healthier. Not money, high achievement or being famous. The big lessons about relationships with family, friends, community and in business are:

- Life is work
- It's not about the number of friends we have or whether or not we're in a committed relationship, it's the quality of our close relationships that matters
- Good relationships don't just protect our bodies, they protect our brains.

Our mobile device might be our remote control to a digital life, but it is face to face relationships that define our health – relationships that we need to humanise, personalise and re-energise at all times, and never take for granted.

Nurture, respect and develop good relationships in all areas of your life.

> There is no bad weather, only inappropriate clothing.
> **Benjamin Zander**

Life is not a rehearsal. Don't expect a big play at the end of your life as life is not a rehearsal. Many people I know seem to have a dream that once they stop working, they will do all the things they ever wanted to do. They have their bucket list ready for when they reach their sixties. Live in the now, and for tomorrow. The journey is the true reward. Be mindful of today.

When people hit their sixties, they will probably have some physical limitations or other constraints, so don't wait. My generation will be working until we're seventy, the next generation will be working until they're eighty.

Life is not a rehearsal. Seize the opportunity, seize the moment, live in the now.

> Curiosity is the engine of achievement.
>
> **Sir Ken Robinson**

Learn, un-learn and re-learn. Be a constant learner, and never stop learning. Start doing some reverse mentoring with the Millennials and Generation Z. Open your mind and be receptive to new things. It's lifelong. It never ends. Be curious. Digital seeing will need to be an everyday play.

'If you only do what you can do, you'll never be better than what you are' – a great quote from Master Shifu in *Kung Fu Panda 3* where he is asking Po, the Kung Fu Panda, to try something different, go outside of his comfort zone, grow and learn a new skill.

Transform your business life

> Nobody said it was easy, no one ever said it would be so hard.
>
> **'The Scientist' by Coldplay**

Find harmony in disharmony. I learned over the years that living in harmony with disharmony can be harmonious. When we're perfectionists, like many people are, we try to harmonise with everything we have – harmony in our inner-circles like family and friends, harmony in our business life and in building relationships with our colleagues. Finding balance in our mental and physical health. Finding harmony in our digital life through Facebook and LinkedIn. Seeking harmony in our personal and business transformation. Keeping up with start-ups and disruptors to develop our businesses. We search for balance in everything we have and do, and all of this demands hard work.

If something is not harmonious, we may get stressed and invest a ton of energy to get everything back to balance, as if reaching an ultimate level of harmony is even feasible. People naively believe this is what they need to be happy, well-respected and have meaning in life. But life is not like this. We need to figure out what's important if we want to survive in this world, control what we control.

We need to start by being comfortable with being uncomfortable. When we reach that point, something happens – that's when we're vulnerable and open for change; open to receiving things that are different. Once we accept this, we will save so much energy, gaining strength and vitality and making us better people. The heaviness of trying to find perfect harmony will soon be replaced by the lightness of living in harmony with disharmony.

Accept the Dualarity of harmony in disharmony and you'll live happily and find peace of mind.

> A strong spirit transcends rules.
>
> **Prince**

Beyond the rules. Of course we have to comply with the laws and rules of our country and our companies, no doubt about that. We don't want to break the law, but we can't live just by the rules. Everything is defined as a process, so be creative. Try reinventing the rules, look to find ways of doing things differently. In my business life, I never took any job description that I had for granted. I created and reinvented it.

Claim your space. If you see something that's not working and there are no rules for it, go out and do something about it.

> **Tintin Snack: musicians break the rules.** Prince embodied breaking the rules with his music. He used intelligence, talent, passion and storytelling in a creative way. He told stories through his music, his performances, and captivated audiences. He changed the rules of the music industry in his fight with Warner Bros, and produced and wrote songs for others.

Try to find a way to make an impact and claim your space.

> Age is an issue of mind over matter. If you don't mind, it doesn't matter.
>
> **Mark Twain**

How older and incumbent can be young and disruptive. There's a great video that shows just how our unconscious biases work called 'Millennials Show Us What "Old" Looks Like'.[127] If you've ever wondered what the Millennials think of the 'old' then watch the YouTube video right to the end. At the start of the video most of them define old as being in your mid-forties, but that perception changes completely at the end. The best part is how it shows that the bond between people is more important than their age – age is just a number. Being old is a mindset or an attitude. On the other side, youngsters need to connect and be open-minded. They still have plenty to learn from the old folks.

When we are open to seeing and learning, and we have energy, age is unimportant. We want to balance between the healthy and the mature. We want to have mixed teams and people so we find the Dualarity. Try doing something non-conventional, as who determines what 'normal' is?

> We don't stop playing because we grow old, we grow old because we stop playing.
>
> **George Bernard Shaw**

Work is life and life is work. I had an aha-moment when I discovered that there is no such thing as work-life balance – work is life and life is work. The perceived work-life balance gives the impression that we only live outside of work and stop living when we work. Work should be life, and if it's not then we have a problem.

Work is a Dualarity where fun, engagement, happiness is equally as important as hard work, targets and results. And in the Fourth Industrial Revolution we ask everyone to perform while they transform, but whatever happens, work has to be life.

If work is not life, change, do something different. At the end of the day, you should have the choice.

> Failure is not the opposite of success, it's a stepping stone.
>
> **Arianna Huffington**

Learn to fail successfully. Benjamin Zander suggests that when you make a mistake, or the people you are working with make a mistake, simply say, 'How fascinating'. By doing this you remove the power of the failure to impact negatively on the opportunity for learning. So next time you miss your budget or your deadline, say, 'How Fascinating'. Why not?

Failure is part of success. If you fail, do it quickly, and more importantly, learn quickly. You never lose; you either win or you learn. You need to fail in order to succeed in your digital transformation.

There are big differences in cultures. In the US failing is more commonly accepted, while in other parts of the world, such as Europe, failing is still not truly seen as part of success. But this is changing, and the start-up movement has bootstrapped the evolution of failure being part of success.

If you fail in business or life never lay blame on others. Remember it's not them, we, I; it is always I first: 'I could have done this better'; 'I should have been on hand'; 'I've done this positively'. Then it's 'We collectively could have done this', and then we start talking about them. We don't talk about the person who didn't do his role or didn't do what we expected because that's the easy part. We get much more energy out of a discussion when blame isn't apportioned.

The CEO of Lego, when evaluating people or leaders who didn't meet their goals, didn't blame them for failing. He blamed them for failing to ask for help and others for failing to give help.

Tintin Snack: I-we-them rule when explaining bad times. During my personal journey I learned the best way to lead is to follow the 'I-we-them' rule when explaining bad times. Never start by blaming others for things that go wrong. Do some self-reflection, then look at your team, your partner, and then look at the things around you where you might not have had any control. Conversely, if things are successful, it's is them, we, then I. Praise your team, your co-workers and then yourself.

We live in an era when nothing can be built to last. Everything is in flux; nothing can sustain. All products, services, markets, and even specific solutions to social problems eventually become obsolete.

When you've built an institution with values and a purpose beyond just making money – when you've built a culture that makes a distinctive contribution while delivering exceptional results – why would you capitulate to the forces of mediocrity and succumb to irrelevance? The best corporate leaders say, 'We are responsible for our results!' No law of nature dictates that a great institution must inevitably fall, at least not within a human lifetime.

Jim Collins, author of many books including *Good To Great*, in his May 2008 article 'The Secret of Enduring Greatness'[128]

The I-we-them rule never fails. And remember, at least you tried if you fail. Learn from it and know it is part of success.

After you plant a seed in the ground, you don't dig it up every week to see how it is doing.

William J Coyne

You can get what you expect without the need to inspect. I truly think we should be able to expect without inspection. If not, then we should question whether we have the right people, the right leaders or even the right culture.

The question should be: 'Why can't I expect without inspection?' Is it our culture that has created this wave of control or is it the past few years where weekly, monthly and quarterly short-term reviews have become the standard? The evolution of productivity tools has pushed us to spend so much time reporting, validating, commenting and showing progress on our green scorecards that it takes up more than 50% of our job. This frustrates the hell out of everyone and often kills any kind of creativity and feeling of personal accountability. We need to challenge the traditional notion of control and centralised power.

Move away from overarching control, operational excellence, scorecard and reviews as your main engine and move towards a culture of giving more trust and learning. Go from a me to a we-collaborative culture. Transition time to report and justify into time to act, talk to customers and be creative with your teams. People need to increase confidence in their abilities and systems. Processes and scorecards are just a support, not a strategy.

Expecting something without inspecting is a sign of ultimate loyalty, commitment, trust and engagement of your people.

> Death is very likely the single best invention of life. It is life's change agent. It clears out the old to make way for the new.
>
> **Steve Jobs**

Give room to newborns. If you imagine the future, there are companies that will disappear and die to make room for something new to be born. There are strategies that will disappear to make room for better ones. There are hierarchies that will be turned upside down to make room for the Millennial mindset of collaboration.

Give room to the newborns in your company.

Dualarity Toolbox

If you only have a hammer, you tend to see every problem as a nail.

Abraham Maslow

Now we've considered some of the principles behind energising ourselves and our businesses, let's look at some tools we can use. These are useful additions to a business repertoire of aids that can help you and your organisation to see what's happening around you and then follow through with actions. Many other tools are available on the market, but I've selected those that reflect the Dualarity and are fuelled by my own learnings.

For more tools and insights go to www.thedualarity.com.

Personal Transformation Toolbox	Business Transformation Toolbox

✓ The Healthy Leader or Person
✓ The Disruptive mindset
✓ Reverse mentoring
✓ Unleash Creativity by Thinking and Doing
✓ Where is your Energy?
✓ Building Your Sparkle Chart
✓ The Art of Gamification
✓ Digital Seeing – Curiosity and Constant Learning are the New DNA
	✓ Transformational Leadership and Cultural Attributes
	✓ Geography Clusters of the Dualarity Genius
	✓ Digital Transformation
	   1. Put Customer Experience At The Heart
	   2. See People as the Soul
	   3. Make Digital the Oxygen of Your Company
	   4. Defining our Purpose – Why and What
	✓ Telling and Selling a Story
	✓ Startups and Incumbents – the best of both Worlds
	✓ A Trendspotting, a Geeks' and a Kids' Board

Personal transformation toolbox

> A healthy mind in a healthy body – Mens sana in corpore sano.
>
> **Juvenalis**

The healthy leader or person. Many industry leaders and authors talk about being a strong, efficient, effective, thoughtful, productive leader or person. So many strategies, rules, approaches and training opportunities are available to support us. But to become such a leader or person, we first need to be healthy, as leadership and wellbeing go hand in hand.

I talk about the golden triangle of a healthy person: sleep, nourishment and exercise.

1   Enough sleep is the starting point, as Arianna Huffington wrote in her new book *The Sleep Revolution: Transforming your life, one night at a time.* Her research showed only 1% of us have the right genes for three to five hours to be enough sleep; the rest of us, 99%, need between seven and nine hours. She talks about being in the middle of a sleep-deprivation crisis impacting every aspect of our health.
2   Physical health is mental health. Invest in your health. Make time to exercise, but don't deprive yourself of sleep in order to do so. Too many people wake up very early to exercise and create their own sleep crisis.
    Exercise is an excellent way to boost our mood and get in shape. When we exercise, our body releases chemicals called endorphins which interact with receptors in our brains that reduce our perception of pain, triggering a positive feeling in the body. This results in an energising outlook on life.

The ancient Greeks did their thinking while walking. Walking gives us energy, refreshes ideas, and we meet people while doing it. At the office, don't sit in your chair the whole day; walk around. Some say sitting is the new smoking. Perhaps install offices without chairs or with only standing desks.

3   And last but not least, find the right nutrition – such as less coffee, less alcohol, more vegetables, fruit and water. The most important meal of the day is breakfast: it strengthens your immune system, slows down ageing and fights cancer. Don't force yourself into a fixed diet as a temporary solution, but eat and drink healthily in a way that you can continue for life. Do everything you do in nutrition with moderation; don't be obsessed by it.

Tintin Snack: burn out – burn in. I lived through a period in the scared quadrant where I was unable to socialise. I was sleepless, stopped doing exercises, was physically present but mentally absent. Every small problem felt like a mountain to climb. I was ashamed of my own condition; I had no sense of humour; the sky always looked dark.

I finally learned to accept where I was and how I was feeling; how I saw the world at that time. Then I communicated with those around me and shared my status, my concerns and that I was open for help. I gained energy by rebuilding relationships with my friends and broader family. Finally, I found the energy to do something about it, take action and move out of the scared quadrant.

I was fortunate that people listened and tried to help me, but ultimately the action had to come from me to activate the change. My lifesaver was sports, and being on the move created oxygen for my brain. I took

all the learnings and symptoms to heart so I would
have a self-warning system for the future.

Make the wellbeing golden triangle of sleep, nutrition and exercise
part of your daily DNA to find the right pace in this accelerating
life. Don't do it out of guilt, but because you believe it necessary to
become the leader that people are waiting for, the one who can
show the path to others. You'll become healthy: the foundation of
personal and business happiness. Do it for your teams, your peers,
your business, your family and friends.

> Millennial isn't a generation, it's a mindset that affects
> people of every age alive today. That mindset comprises
> three values: individuality, global connectedness, and
> purpose.
>
> **Philippe von Borries, Co-founder and Co-CEO, Refinery29**

The disruptive mindset. If you want to become a Millennial-type
company, you don't need to hire an army of Millennials. Have the
mindset of Millennials, seeing the world as one big playground.
They don't see the confines or the narrowness of things.

Every single start-up thinks it has the best idea. Some are run by
Millennials, and it's amazing the appetite they have, but also the
naivety they have. They're not bound by rules, processes or layers,
and that is incredibly important. So partner with them, hire some
of them, and importantly, change your own mindset.

Author, *Harvard Business Review* blogger and consultant Whitney
Johnson walks us through her seven-step model in her Lynda.com
course from LinkedIn 'Disrupting Yourself' and move to the next
level in your career,[129] explaining how to take high risks, play to
our strengths and embrace constraints, letting go of the past while
bringing the learnings with us.

To stay competitive and thrive in today's world, companies need to release expectations from the past. To open themselves to entirely new mindsets about what their brand means. To let their very identity evolve. The same is true for you.

Erica Ariel Fox, New York Times Bestselling
Author of Winning from Within

What you can do:

- Connect those with a disruptive mindset to those without one
- Partner with people who have Millennial mindsets and change your own mindset.

Disrupting yourself is the secret to breaking into a new field, never settling for less and achieving more. Disrupting yourself first will help you to transform others.

Tell me and I forget, teach me and I may remember, involve me and I learn.

Benjamin Franklin

Reverse mentoring. To help us to have better digital cross-learning in our organisations we can install a reverse mentoring programme. This is nothing new, but it is back on the list in the Digital Revolution. Instead of assuming the wisest people are the oldest, most experienced and most mature, get younger people to mentor the less digital savvy. This goes against more established workplace practices, but the new world of the fast and furious demands a new approached to mentoring.

Millennials see things we might not see. They probably have more energy and are usually in the healthy quadrant, and this is contagious. Digital wisdom can then be shared with people lacking insights and digital seeing which will bridge the gap between the generations, give new energy and confidence to the older generation, and increase retention of the younger generation. It supports the idea that learning never ends.

When we start reverse mentoring as a mentee we want insights on the following things:

1 Find a reverse mentoring sparring partner, either inside or outside the company, who you believe reflects the new world best. Ideally have one internal and one external mentor
2 Be honest about your own goals for the mentoring. Have an open mind and be receptive to a different style of communication. And don't forget that the mentee sets the boundaries of the feedback from the mentor in the way they react to it.
3 Try to find answers to:
   a What can you do to use and leverage the latest in technology, social media and current trends in innovation better?
   b What does it mean to be digitally cool today?
   Share your plans or thoughts on digital and ask for feedback on them
4 Make sure your mentor(s) learn new things from you.

> You can be creative in anything – in maths, science, engineering, philosophy – as much as you can in music or in painting or in dance.
>
> **Sir Ken Robinson**

Unleashing creativity by thinking and doing. As we live in a world that celebrates rushing and being busy – busyness – we need to find moments and places to think. When we have too many things to do, we lack time to think and be creative. In his talk on Unleashing Creativity,[130] John Cleese advocates actually planning thinking moments, slowing down, making space literally and figuratively, enjoying the silent moments.

Tintin Snack: movies unleash creativity. Movies are a terrific canvas for storytelling and unleashing creativity. These three films have had a huge impact on me: *Silence of the Lambs, Lord of the Rings*, and *Avatar*. They have a few things in common: amazing stories, visual perfection, rhythm and pace, beautiful music. When we have this combination of senses activated at the same time, we can be transported into a new creative realm, captivated.

Find a space in or outside your office where you and your employees can go to be quiet. Make it a sacred space, calming and relaxing, away from disturbances – a no-digital zone! Go there yourself, and encourage your employees to go there when they need space to think and be creative. Even better is to dedicate a room that you could call 'The Inspiration Room' with some relaxing seats, optional music and walls that can be written on.

Plan thinking days or thinking moments in your agenda for yourself and your team. They are sacred, so don't postpone or use them for operational work. Don't make them short term either. They need to be for the long-term.

Where is your energy? By asking people two very simple questions, we will learn more in a couple of minutes than we would in deep dive discussions or meet and greet sessions.

The two questions are:

1   What gives you energy?
2   What takes energy away from you?

That's it. The answers will give us a clear understanding about why someone is performing and enjoying their work, or why they aren't happy. When we have the answers to these two questions, we can strengthen the things that they have energy for or move them on to something that will give them energy. They can make a choice, and we can help them reorient themselves if their energy drain is higher than their energy gain. Energy plus has to be bigger than energy minus, otherwise we have a problem.

It's the same with relationships. 'What gives me energy in a relationship? What takes energy away?'

Examples of energy giving could be, 'I love to have speaking opportunities'; 'I love owning personal projects'; 'I love to listen to music when I work'; 'I love cooking'; 'I love off-sites'; 'I love pleasing, helping to solve problems'; 'I love social marketing'. Energy taking examples could be: 'I have too many internal meetings without clear goals'; 'I'm reporting every day'; 'I'm being managed too closely'; 'I'm not part of a real team'.

> **Tintin Snack: the emotional La.** I learned from André Pelgrims about the emotional La (La from Do, Re, Mi, Fa, Sol, La, Si, Do). When our partners have a lot of stress in their work, they come home and start complaining. This removes all the good positive energy from the room and determines the mood of the rest of the evening, and often the mood worsens. The emotional La means that when we arrive home, we find a way of not talking about work. Or we use the car journey to cool down so by the time we are home, we are more zen-like. Our heart rate goes down which gives us an emotional cooling down period. So some commute time might not be so bad after all.

Some people are uncomfortable with expressing emotion about their dreams, but it's the passion and emotion that will attract and motivate others.

Jim Collins

Building your sparkle chart. My number one criterion when hiring someone is not to look at their business or educational background, but to look for the sparkle in their eyes. The same applies when meeting new people. In French there is a beautiful expression *'Les yeux qui pétillent'*. To grow and to be happy, we need to find sparkle at home and at work. Without it, we are just living a life. Nothing more, nothing less.

Find your purpose and you will find your sparkle.

So how do we make people sparkle in an organisation? If they have lost their sparkle, why is this?

We create a sparkle chart for individuals and consolidate common themes as a group, especially if performing while transforming is demanding so much of people that they are getting buried under to-dos and must-dos. There are four steps:

Step 1: what are my roadblocks? In order to scale or sparkle, we need to make sure we address the current roadblocks. We ask people in group or as individuals to table the current roadblocks in their job and write them on Post-its. Then we divide them into groups of things in our control and those out of our control. The ones we don't control will be driven by what I would call an influence strategy, meaning we can give feedback or influence people who do have control. On each roadblock we write owners and timelines to address them. This is the outside circle.

Step 2: how do I scale? The second thing we need is to find scale in our current job and organisation. We have finite time at work, we have finite resources, so how do we scale? What are the things we can do, such as leveraging an ecosystem, determining programmatic approaches or partners, changing meeting rhythms, engaging with start-ups, leveraging events, or selling/telling our story to others to get support and momentum? How can strengths become even stronger? And what will we do differently to scale? This is the second circle.

Step 3: what is my sparkle? What will make us sparkle at the end of the year? What are the things that will make us proud? What is the thing that will make us shine and say, 'I feel really energised'? We can ask each individual and do this as a group. This is the third circle.

Step 4: are there any patterns? The last step is to see if there are patterns and see where we can group ideas, outcomes and people together. Some might just be relevant for individuals or specific teams.

The benefits of this process are huge and have deep impact. By creating the sparkle chart with our colleagues, we not only help ourselves, but it's also a kind of therapy session. If we do this in groups, people feel relieved that they have been able to talk about their roadblocks. They feel appreciated because others have heard what is inhibiting their performance. Everyone understands each other better.

This whole exercise can be done around a specific subject or theme, like digital transformation, customer experience, IoT, etc.

We can also start at a company level with all managers. As an outcome we can define three to six predominant things that become cross-divisional projects. Specific things will remain with us and the manager.

Put the sparkle chart as part of your dialogue and discussion with individuals and make sure that you keep it top of mind when doing reviews or connecting with managers or employees.

One of the key roles of a manager is to make people succeed by removing roadblocks. What is it that keeps them awake at night because they can't find a solution? How can we help them scale? How can we help them sparkle? If they sparkle, we all sparkle, and that will release a lot of energy.

The art of gamification. Gamification is going to be more present in many parts of our life, not because it's the hot new thing, but because it's proven to work for many. It will be valuable to instil this in education and business so people can be creative and play with technology.

Let's zoom in on some gaming innovations that teach coding and how to be creative with tech.

Minecraft, a Swedish computer game purchased by Microsoft in 2014, enables players to build creative constructions in a colourful 3D world. The Minecraft generation has more than 40 million monthly users and has sold more than 100 million copies. In 2011, MinecraftEdu made its way into thousands of classrooms around the world to teach skills from maths to foreign languages to fair trade. Recently Minecraft launched a site specifically for teachers to share tips on how to use it in the classroom.

Another great example in education is Mindstorm from Lego that contains hardware and software to create customisable and pro-grammable robots. Apple recently launched the Swift Playground app for kids to learn to program in a fun way.

For families, I came across the London based start-up company SAM Labs, creating modular kits and wireless blocks connected to an app to teach all ages to learn and connect with the IoT and play with tech. It's very much child's play, but I believe it could be useful for businesses to help connect less digital savvy people with tech.

> **Tintin Snack: connected Internet of Things.** During a conference I enjoyed a simple workshop on how to combine a product and a service to create an IoT object. It was a great way of proving that anyone can innovate. We sat together in groups of five to ten people and were asked, 'Let's take a pen (object) and a restaurant (service). Can you make an IoT product by combining both?' Within half an hour we had more than five creative IoT ideas which showed that everyone can be creative in the right environment – we had a legal counsel at our table who didn't know he could be creative.

You find innovative connected IoT solutions when you put creativity to work.

Create a gamifying way of enjoying technology and the IoT at work, at home or in schools. The fastest way of having fun with technology is to become creative again.

> In the future, the defining metric for organizations won't be ROI (Return on Investment), but ROL (Return on Learning).
>
> Salim Ismail, author of the *Exponential Organizations: Why new organizations are ten times better, faster, and cheaper than yours*

Digital seeing – curiosity and content learning are the new DNA. When we are curious and constantly learning, we will be able to see what's happening around us. We can read books, go to workshops, watch speakers – whatever works, but we have to keep seeing. We need to lean forward ourselves and consciously want to learn. The future successful people are not the ones who know today but the ones who learn for tomorrow.

Don't overload yourself with too much information. Be selective.

Here are some of the best resources I use to be up to date, in the know. They're available to help you see what's happening in the digital, personal and business development arenas.

World Economic Forum – www.weforum.org. This is a global institute of around 600 original thinkers who are connected around the world with people from politicians to professors, from start-ups to incumbents in any industry. They write reports around everything that is happening, from short 500 word briefings to everything you'd want to know about a certain subject, making predictions about technology, geographic changes, etc. You can select articles and create a sequence, like a book.

TED – www.ted.com. Some of the best presentations in the world can be found on the TED.com website or app. TED (Technology, Entertainment and Design) is a non-profit organisation devoted to spreading ideas worth spreading, usually in the form of short, powerful talks of eighteen minutes or fewer. What I've noticed about the best TED talks is that they have unique content to share. They shoot for the heart, capture the mind and most of them make people smile.

There's a great book by Carmine Gallo, *The Storyteller's Secret*,[131] which analyses 500 of the best TED talks to find out what they had in common. The author notes that with the new paradigm of social and economic connectivity, communication skills and ideas are the currency of today. He says that by mastering the skills of communication, we will be able to 'astonish, electrify and inspire our audience'. TED's strapline is 'ideas worth sharing' – and they are worth spreading.

The Automated Economy – www.facebook.com/TheAutomated Economy. If you want to know how the economy will be automated over time, this is a great little-known source. It's useful because it scans the surface of automation. If you want to know how your business, your manufacturing plant, or your receptionist will be automated, it gives you examples.

Singularity University – singularityu.org. Some of the smartest minds based in Silicon Valley come together. They are the leading thinkers about the future providing educational programmes, innovative partnerships and a start-up accelerator to help individuals, businesses, institutions, investors, NGOs and governments understand cutting-edge technologies, and how to use them to impact billions of people positively.

www.futurism.com is interesting because it covers the breakthrough technologies that will shape humanity's future.

www.medium.com and **LinkedIn** are great places for articles. And **www.mintel.com** is the world's leading market intelligence agency. **www.statista.com** is one of the world's largest statistics portals.

Leading thinkers and trend watchers. People like Brian Solis, Thomas Frey, Patrick Dixon www.globalchange.com/, Ray Kurzweil, Gerd Leonhard are trend watchers you can follow. Select leading thinkers and useful channels on LinkedIn Pulse to follow. I'd also recommend you read the famous yearly *Internet Trends Report* from Mary Keeper on www.kpcb.com/internet-trends.

The Center for the Study of Digital Life (CSDL)digitallife.center is a non- profit strategic research group dedicated to understanding the effects of digital technologies on civilisations, both East and West, led by futurologist Mark Stahlman. Our future will depend on the play between West, East and the digital.

You can keep an eye on the digital transformation information shared by **the most prestigious consulting firms**[132] like McKinsey & Company, Bean & Company, The Boston Consulting Group Inc., Accenture, Deloitte Consulting, Booz Allen Hamilton, Ernst & Young, PWC, AT Kearney, IBM Global Services and KPMG. Check the new breeds of service companies in the digital world like Duval Union, You and Mr Jones, The Business Innovator Factory and many others around the world.

And of course you can follow The Dualarity on LinkedIn, Facebook or **www.thedualarity.com**

It's all about leaning forward. Sign up for newsletters, be selective and find ways to keep up, to keep seeing.

For more great trend watching sources go to my website www.thedualarity.com.

Business transformation toolbox

> We need more people doing digital, fewer people in the
> digital team.
>
> Amanda Neylon, Head of Digital, Macmillan Cancer Support

Transformational leadership and cultural attributes. If we look at what's happening in the business world all around us, we realise that we need to balance performing and transforming. We'll talk about the cultural attributes and the leadership capabilities we have to develop as companies to enable transformation and performance at the same time. Digital is fundamentally changing how business gets done; it's the oxygen of companies.

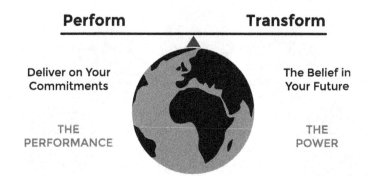

Perform — Deliver on Your Commitments — THE PERFORMANCE

Transform — The Belief in Your Future — THE POWER

The transforming while performing balance is very tough. We need to perform and deliver on our commitments: improve profit, excel on the scorecards, deliver shareholder value, create happy customers, deliver on time, grow the business, improve margin and take market share. Transformation on the other hand is the power that drives us forward, the belief in our future. This is why people will buy our shares and employees will remain loyal and inspired.

Analysts, shareholders, customers, employees want to see your power and ability to transform, so ask yourself:

- Am I able to lead the company? Am I able to transform myself so I can transform my business? Am I able to transform and keep performing for the short term?
- Am I able to define the vision? What are the why and what?
- Can I put in place a successful strategy?

People want to believe in our future. Employees stay in companies they believe have a future. To be able to transform while performing we need the right culture, attributes and leadership. We need to create a culture of transformation.

Culture eats strategy for breakfast, lunch, and dinner.

Peter Drucker

At the end of the day it's all about the culture. An article on the journey of Nelson Mandela inspired me to map my experience into ten steps to transformational leadership. The advice works for companies, small and large, and individuals, and helps us think about how we can make the change to perform and transform.

Transformation might take years. It never ends, but today's pressure and pace means transformation is bigger and faster than ever. Cultural transformations are seldom cost-free and demand energy and attention.

These ten steps are needed to transform while performing:

1. Create a coalition of the willing. We have to build a transformation team independent of hierarchies. To create a culture that can transform, we need change agents across the organisation at all levels: a coalition of the willing and the capable. They are the ones who understand what needs to happen; they are willing; they have energy; they see. They create a forum to foster a kernel of enthusiasm that in the long run becomes contagious so more in the organisation will join.

Every organisation has change agents who energise others. Create a band of brothers and sisters to lead the transformation, extend it and infect others with their enthusiasm as time goes by. If people don't want to join, it is because we haven't invited them to the table. Find the Dualarity heroes that can transform and perform.

2. Build a future-proof organisation. We have to think about the skillsets to develop internally and which we need to hire to complement what we have. Then we make sure the incumbents don't fear for their jobs, don't fear we'll replace them with younger digital natives. The incumbents have experience and skills that, with some tweaks, training, reversed mentoring and continuous learning, could become the sparkling jewels of our businesses. It is vital to infuse digital skills in all people within the organisation.

Senior leadership has to create the right conditions for the transformation and hire and closely involve the right middle management, so critical in driving the change as they're close to the customer. As Jonas Ridderstrale and Kjell Anders Nordstrom, Swedish economists and authors, point out in one of their books *Funky Business – Talent makes capital dance*

On the leadership front, hiring a chief digital officer (CDO) is often the first step for many organisations. When doing so, it is critical we position the role at the appropriate level in the organisation, with sufficient scope, influence and sponsorship to make change happen. We need to hire a chief design officer (also CDO) with the right mindset to lead the design strategy, map the customer journeys and leverage human-centric design research approaches to connect with customers. Other roles are beginning to emerge such as chief data officers, chief analytics officers and chief growth or monetisation officers. And in many cases the role of a chief marketing officer with strong digital and business skills will grow in importance, in some cases becoming the CMDO, while the CIO will need to decide where to go and how to evolve.

CEOs should avoid behaving like politicians by focusing on the short term even though most of these roles only have an average lifespan of six to seven years, while a CFO has five to six years and a marketer less than that. British WPP media icon Sir Martin Sorrel says that the Top 500 Standard & Poors (S&P) companies paid more money on dividends and buying their own shares than they made in profits. This means that a board of directors should resist Wall Street and focusing on short term performance, instead looking at the innovative character of the long term and keeping their CEOs longer. We need to encourage mature Dualarity Quadrant employees to avoid complacency and move towards a healthy attitude.

The hierarchies as we know them today have their history in the First Industrial Revolution, created to help organisations expand in a structured way. And maybe over time we might see fewer chiefs when roles blend and organisational structures evolve to reflect the new revolution, the new generations, where static hierarchies will become more dynamic. Structures that are less strict, less focused on control and efficiency but more agile, networked and dynamic, will respond to today's world of the fast and furious. Organisations that are structured and networked more around projects or themes are breaking down and bridging company boundaries.

3. Define a compelling purpose. Digital transformation on its own is not a good enough purpose. We need to define an inspiring purpose and answer why we are starting this change, and the reason has to be compelling so that people feel they're part of the bigger purpose. It can't just be because others are doing it.

4. Think like a customer. Thinking like a customer is not the same as thinking about the customer or customer experience. It's not inside out, but outside in. We need to put ourselves in their shoes, show empathy with the customer because they're much more vocal and informed than ever before. They have more choice, and can change more rapidly because of the technology at hand and the insights available on any company. However, we must avoid saying we are customer obsessed as no one wants us to be obsessed with them. It is a scary thought.

More importantly we need to create a culture that makes data-based decisions. Decisions should not be based on experiences or what we believe the customer wants, but should be challenged with data insights and predictions. This will probably influence how we operate and are organised. Design with the user at heart as bad experiences are memorable, but great experiences make fans. Make it a frictionless customer experience fuelled by insights and personalisation.

5. Inspire with action and authenticity. It is important to be authentic in our actions. We need authenticity at every level of the organisation and from each individual. To inspire with our actions might mean we roll up our sleeves and get stuck into the transformation. We mustn't delegate digital transformation, it's not a standard change management. We have to engage by being authentic. It's difficult for people to make these changes, so showing our own struggles helps everyone come along. And this has to start at the level of senior management.

So what will your personal authenticity in the transformation be? Don't play a role because management ask you to do so; don't be an actor as that drains a lot of energy. Do it because you believe in it. Enough talk – lead with authenticity and act on it.

> How do we turn all this sector talk into sector action?
>
> **Emma Thomas, former CEO Youthnet**

6. Foster a culture of fail fast and learn fast. These days we can't have projects that take five years to complete and cost millions of euros. We have to fail fast and learn from it, but we need to learn fast. Failing is not the opposite of success, failing is part of success. We rebuild and reinvent. Foster an environment and culture where experimentation is part of the normal. Learn to fail successfully. This is the culture embodied in the healthy quadrant of the Dualarity.

> In a world that's changing really quickly, the only strategy that is guaranteed to fail is not taking risks.
>
> **Taken from an October 2011 interview at Y Combinator's start-up school in Palo Alto, California**

7. Enjoy field journalism. We need to communicate, communicate and communicate. Communicate success and failure, allow people to see where progress is being made and where it is not. Give them a perspective on the short term and long term results, an outlook on when hard work will give dividends and how far the light at the end of the tunnel is. They need to believe it is not a flight of fancy, so we need to communicate very clearly the why and what is in it for them.

Dare to say what you think, with respect, even if people might not want to hear it. When we have a coalition of the willing, we're contagious. People will want to join. Show signs that things are working and be transparent about failures. Don't wait all year to have a big splash and celebrate success. With transformation, successes and failures might be small and often. Communicate them all directly through your coalition and great storytelling, which I will address later on.

8. Create a culture of an open mindset. With a growth and collaborative mindset we allow innovation to flourish. It is the mindset that matters, regardless of age or occupation. Stanford University psychologist and Professor Carol Dweck, author of *Mindset*, has described people with a growth mindset as those who believe that ability can be developed. They believe in persistence in the face of setbacks, seeing failures as essential to mastery, learning from criticism, embracing challenges with agility, and finding lessons and inspiration in the success of others. Those with fixed mindsets give up easily, see failures as scary, ignore useful negative feedback, avoid challenges, don't believe they can change.

With a growth mindset we develop, we are less stressed and more creative. Trying to be creative as an end goal is not the right way to go. Setting the right conditions is what should prevail. Be open minded and see the world ahead as one full of opportunities and learnings.

9. Remain focused on your North Star. We mustn't lose our North Star. If we spend too much energy on the non-believers, trying to drag them along, the believers might get confused as they get less attention and feel things are slowing down. If the non-believers don't join us, open their mindset and become willing to learn, we replace them with people who do.

10. Transform yourself so you can transform others, lead yourself so you can lead others.

> **Tintin Snack: avoid the 'no, but, however' people.** These people always have a 'no', 'but,' or 'however' to add to the conversation. They have fixed mindsets, are innovation, energy and conversation killers. Marshall Goldsmith, prolific best-selling author of *What Got You Here Won't Get You There*, suggest that we not only monitor our colleagues for this fixed mindset tendency, but that we monitor our own language too.

The world will be divided not just between the strong and the weak or the rich and the poor, but between the learners who are open to change their abilities and the non-learners with fixed mindsets. Open your mind, create a culture of transformation and explore the world outside of your comfort zone. Explore the Dualarity.

> A Talent hits a target no one else can hit; a Genius hits a target no one else can see.
>
> **Arthur Schopenhauer**

Geographic clusters of the Dualarity genius. What defines a creative genius like Aristotle, Plato, Mozart, Da Vinci or Steve Jobs, and why do certain places at certain moments in time burst with creative genius? Why do places become hubs of cultural, political and technological prosperity? The American Journalist and author Eric Weiner wrote a very interesting book called *The Geography Of Genius* to try to answer these questions.

He selected seven clusters, places of genius, for his research and wrote his story by making seven stops across the world: Athens (from Socrates to Aristotle), Hangzhou (flourishing Song Dynasty as the centre of science and poetry), Florence (art during the Renaissance under the Medicis), Edinburgh (the Scottish Enlightenment modern medical advances), Calcutta (chaos spurring creativity), Vienna (centre of music in the age of Mozart and a centre of art and psychology in the age of Freud) and San Francisco (the Silicon Valley) and discovered that we get the geniuses we deserve. Music was hot in the 18th century so we got Beethoven, Bach and Mozart in Vienna. Technology is admired today so we get Bill Gates, Elon Musk, Steve Jobs and Mark Zuckerberg, even though most of them never finished their academic studies.

So why is this? What do they have in common? By incorporating some of the following learnings we can get the best out of our teams or grow a part of our organisation to be healthy or mature. We can create the conditions for genius to find its place and develop.

1. A level of chaos unleashes creativity and sparks imagination – not anarchy, but a level of instability and intrigue, risk-taking and openness to experience. Obsession for operational excellence might not be good for every part of our business; getting closer to some kind of entrepreneurial chaos is good for us so we unleash the creative energy and ideas. We can test things out without reaching for excellence when failure is an option and the learning that comes with it is the reward. Encourage people away from the scared quadrant and show them that a level of chaos can be healthy.

2. Diversity and a collision of cultures means an open tolerance for experiences and ideas such as sea ports, internet, open immigration. Today 50% of start-ups in San Francisco are headed by non-US born people. Having a diverse workforce blending different generations and mindsets is essential. Scared quadrant thinkers might feel threatened by diversity, so help them achieve a mature state of mind.

3. Good judgement – to distinguish bad ideas from good ideas. We can do this by seeing and understanding what is happening and leveraging data for decision-making. And we do our best thinking while walking around. Here our maturity can be a real asset.

4. Room for conflict – freedom of speech, places for public debate. Respect different opinions and encourage feedback from customers and employees. Handle feedback as a gift. Allow conflict without fear; enable the scared or injured to move into the healthy quadrant.

5. Systems of mentorship. Find a good mentor, install a sustainable mentoring programme, and even better, consider reverse mentorship. Mentorship can be a way of leading people out of the scared and injured zones into the light of maturity and health.

6. Many geniuses borrow from others. They appropriate other people's ideas then perfect them. Being innovative doesn't mean you need to invent something.

To foster genius, we of course need some money, and we need to use that money to enable creativity. Most geniuses came from the middle-class not from the rich; genius is part of a culture that grows organically. The clusters of genius disappear when some of the above ingredients disappear, for example in Athens when the immigration politics changed. San Francisco is starting to show some signs of reduction in genius as too many are showing-off with their money. Most often complacency and arrogance drive the disappearance as the genius cluster matures, with each cluster surviving less than a full century.

We can see that mature companies who have their own genius cluster could fall foul of the complacency and arrogance problem.

A key lesson is not to copy the clusters of genius. Many cities try to copy the success of Silicon Valley, a former farming area. It didn't invent new things like the transistor (New Jersey), mobile phones (Illinois), Internet (Switzerland) and venture capital (New York); it perfected inventions. San Francisco is where good ideas learned to walk. Many cities are fighting to become the next San Francisco and have innovation hubs, like Rockstart in Amsterdam, Betahaus in Berlin, Numa in Paris, and in Belgium Ghent, Antwerp and Brussels are fighting for the title in Europe. However, cities inside a country should unify their efforts, like StartupDelta where Amsterdam, Den Haag and Eindhoven have joined forces and became one of the Top 20 global start-up ecosystems. The Netherlands organised a world-class start-up Fest Europe event in May 2016 and succeeded, by leveraging former European Dutch commissioner Neelie Kroes, to attract top CEOs of the tech world from Apple, Uber and Google. Only Davos has been able to do this in the past, so this could set the Netherlands ahead of all other European countries as a start-up epicentre.

Tintin Snack: creativity as a driver for economic and social development![133] A 2015 study by the Martin Prosperity Institute.[134] titled 'The Global Creativity Index 2015', presents a new model of economic development making the link between creativity and economic development by looking at three Ts: talent, technology and tolerance. Technology – research and development investment, and patents per capita. Talent – share of adults with higher education and workforce in the creative class. Tolerance – treatment of immigrants, racial and ethnic minorities, gays and lesbians. It mapped 139 countries using these benchmarks.

If you want to know whether your city will be a healthy, mature, injured or scared city, have a look at where you are today and what you can do to improve creativity and attract talent.

Rank	Country	Technology	Talent	Tolerance	Global Creativity Index
1	Australia	7	1	4	0.970
2	United States	4	3	11	0.950
3	New Zealand	7	8	3	0.949
4	Canada	13	14	1	0.920
5	Denmark	10	6	13	0.917
6	Finland	5	3	20	0.917
7	Sweden	11	8	10	0.915
8	Iceland	26	2	2	0.913
9	Singapore	7	5	23	0.896
10	Netherlands	20	11	6	0.889
11	Norway	18	12	9	0.883
12	United Kingdom	15	20	5	0.881
13	Ireland	23	21	7	0.845
14	Germany	7	28	18	0.837
15	Switzerland	19	22	17	0.822
16	France	16	26	16	0.822
17	Slovenia	17	8	35	0.822
18	Belgium	28	18	14	0.817
19	Spain	31	19	12	0.811
20	Austria	12	26	32	0.788
21	Hong Kong	32	32	30	0.715
22	Italy	25	31	38	0.715
23	Portugal	35	36	22	0.710
24	Japan	2	58	39	0.708
25	Luxembourg	20	48	32	0.696

Source study by the Martin Prosperity Institute,
titled the Global Creativity Index 2015

Digital transformation. Digital transformation isn't just about hiring a CDO, starting some projects and hoping for the best. The three pillars we've talked about before are the foundations for your digital transformation strategy.

Start with the customer experience and then have technology work on it.

Steve Jobs

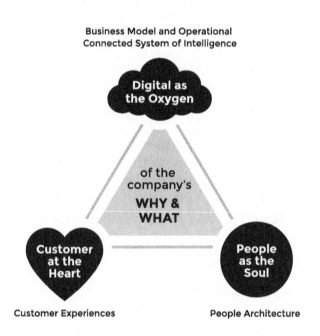

Put customer experience at the heart. Today, of course we need a good product and good service to be successful in business, but the *customer experience* is even more important – a dynamic customer journey with magic micro-moments in it. Each step on a customer experience, from the first moment they hear about the product, the ordering experience, the delivery, using the product, the co-creation, the reactive and proactive service to finally re-ordering, is important. And it doesn't end there. There's also the information that follows, aftercare and service, support issues, product returns and refunds. The whole frictionless experience is what people remember. It is how we made them feel, not what we promised or did. If they have a bad experience even with a good product, they will not come back. If the experience works, they will be willing to pay a premium for it, and in the ideal case become a brand ambassador and ultimately a real fan going beyond just being satisfied. And this fan can be a consumer, customer, partner or citizen.

A fundamental part of the customer experience is the product or the service itself. The digital revolution can give us creative ideas for product innovations and designs. Both Apple and Dyson have understood this very well as they designed their product with the user at the heart. They have people-centric products and services.

Give customers a voice in the boardroom and at the user design-room tables. Let them flex their creative muscles and be part of the development of new products and services. Organise hackathons for start-ups, customers and employees where entrepreneurs and tech people come together for one or two days to hack innovative ideas that can be launched at start-up speed. This can play a valuable role in accelerating the digital transformation and infuse more innovation driven mindsets within organisations.

The on-demand generation wants a responsive, relevant and transparent economy. They share their experiences rapidly. Be where they are, at the right moment and in the right context. When you empower the customer and put them at the heart of each transaction, put them in control of their own buying journey and create networked customer communities, loyalty and satisfaction will rise.

By truly understanding your customer, their needs, their intentions and behaviours through utilising the power of digital, you will garner customer loyalty.

> Digital insights are the new currency of business.
> **Forrester Research**

With the information systems and technology available, you can give your customers a great experience. So put your data to work to deliver the best digital experience, one where you deliver a tailored personalised and individualised experience by shifting from customer-centricity to personal-centricity. If you do that, data will become a massive source of revenue and fuel your monetisation.

In summary, customers will in many cases prioritise the experience of buying and using your product over the performance of that product. Designing your user strategies to connect with customers is growing and becoming central in your customer experiences.

Great examples are Disney's new admission bracelet that tracks every step a visitor takes and uses the data to design a more fluid customer experience. With each drink purchased, Coke's new vending machine (co-designed by Apple's former senior designer) captures data, allowing Coke to tap into previously unseen consumer behaviour patterns.

We can no longer buy attention, we have to earn it by putting the customer at the heart of the company. And it is not thinking about customers that will work, but thinking like customers.

Ask yourself:

1 How can I create a phenomenal customer experience? Is it a *frictionless experience*? And what is my user design strategy?
2 What do I need to do to make my customers turn into *fans*? Do I truly understand their needs, wants and behaviours? How can I show my customers that they are at the heart of everything I do by having a personalised approach, embedding their feedback from all channels and involving them in my offerings?
3 Are my design and customer experience metrics adjusted to my strategy? Can I track them through *real-time data systems*?

This is not just a question of changing skillset. It is a changing of mindset.

Julie Dodd, author of *The New Reality*

See people as the soul. People are the soul of the company. They are the architecture. Culturally a lot is happening, so we need people performing as well as transforming. How do we attract the right people, keep them, and help them feel happy and optimistic about the changes that are happening all around them? Do they understand technology? Do we have the right talent in-house, or do we need to hire? Do we need to re-hire current talent? We need to think about the organisation we want that is future-proof.

Training and education need to become proactive to help modernise the workforce, creating a culture of continual learning and creativity. Programmes need to be developed to work on the mindset in the organisation and reflect the why and what of the company. Improving happiness and engagement between employees and employer will become essential to attract and retain the talent. The battle for talent is at your back.

> The main obstacles for businesses looking for rapid digital transformation[135] relate to company culture, organizational complexity and the lack of processes that enable employees to engage, collaborate and innovate.
>
> **Research from Bizagi, a digital process automation software vendor**

With the rise of digital natives as Generations Y and Z join the workforce, there will be a shift in the organisational demographics. A new type of HR professional is needed to provide a workplace that is welcoming to the Millennials and their mindset and can see the opportunities these connected and engaged collaborators bring. Reward teams more than the individual to foster collaboration and communication while breaking down organisational boundaries, remaining connected to the collective identity of the organisation.

New roles like algorithmists and data scientists will be created and old ones will be destroyed. Static hierarchies will change into dynamic hierarchies, the purpose economy will drive Dualarity entrepreneurship, and the start-up mentality will be celebrated.

Many roles within the organisation and the dynamics between employer and employee are changing. Freelancing is a new flexible way of working. The nine-to-five job is changing to reflect the twenty-four hour on-demand economy.

Ask yourself:

1   Where are the *Dualarity heroes* in my organisation? I will re-hire them, invite them to join the next chapter. Do I have a coalition of the willing in place? Is my organisation and culture future-proof? Do I need to hire new talent or find new networks of partnerships? Do I have the three critical roles in place, the digital, design and data officers?

2   Do I have a *life-long learning* programme in place for my people? Are my digital skills well spread in the organisation? Do I organise hackathons to blend generations and foster digital ideation? Is my workplace adapting new ways of working leveraging the newest technology so people feel empowered?

3   What ways do I *reward* and honour the people who manage to transform and continue performing? Do I reward cross-boundary collaboration enough?

> Digital is the transformation agent, not the transformation.
>
> **Gerry McGovern**

Make digital the oxygen of your company. When we understand that digital is the oxygen of our company, that without it our business cannot survive, and how digital goes through the whole business model and operations, we find ourselves balanced in the Dualarity.

Just as oxygen is essential, digital technologies are essential to our lives as informed citizens, consumers, creators, leaders and business owners. The digital oxygen supports transformation, our life personally and our ecosystem at work and at home.

Using technology to understand, manage and align our value chain, customer segments, revenue streams, channels, key partners, processes, resources, activities, cost structure, product innovation and customer relationships better provides us with competitive advantage. Taking advantage of new types of innovation, like the IoT, big data and artificial intelligence, we create interconnected systems of intelligence in our organisations that will improve our performance. By balancing operational excellence with the disruption and chaos that digital technology brings, we will ensure our longevity and creativity. We will find balance in the Dualarity of performing while transforming.

Digital transformation needs to be strategic, focused on the short term and long term. It should not be seen as tactical, fed by a me-too approach resulting in a few projects that are innovative but don't fit the long term strategy.

Digital is the enabler. It is not a target or a means to an end. It is the oxygen of the company; without it we cannot do business.

Consider:

1 Is my digital transformation strategy supported at the company level and seen as a strategic versus a me-too tactical approach? Is senior management creating the *conditions* (people, digital, customer experience, why and what) to succeed in this journey? What kind of budgets are available? Do they still sit in the traditional 10% innovation budget allocation?

2 Do I have *real-time 'source of truth' analytics* generating insights available for my people and the key decision-makers? Do I have a clear privacy and security strategy in place across the organisation, and do I give my customers the right level of transparency about how I use their data?

3 Are the less strict *business outcomes and monetisation models* defined, even if they might not be as clear due to the speed of the changes (remember fail fast, learn fast)? Are my digital processes, operations and business model in line with my digital strategy? How can chaotic disruption benefit my business processes?

4 What new technology could impact quickly on my standard procedures?

Defining our purpose – our why. Defining the why is about capturing the minds and hearts of people so we can do business with and attract those who have the same beliefs as us. Most often when we define our why we find our how and what. This applies to individuals as well as businesses.

Ask yourself: 'Why do I get out of bed every day? Why do I go to work every day? What is my cause or belief? Why do I do what I do? Why does my business exist? Why do I live?'

Gaining market share or making profits are not whys but goals or outcomes. The why has to be inspirational and capture the heart before it captures the mind. People want to find purpose for their lives so they buy from companies that have a magical purpose they can be part of. A clear purpose will help you to put your energy where it matters and be entrepreneurial, keeping focus and surprising your customers.

Simon Sinek's work, and that of other experts, is a great resource if you want to go deeper.

Tell me the facts and I'll learn. Tell me the truth and I'll believe. But tell me a story and it will live in my heart for ever.

An old Native American proverb

Telling and selling a story. Storytelling for individuals and business people is all about connecting with others and helping them to see what we see, then bringing them along on our journey and energising them. When we tell a story to our partner, a business colleague, an important investor, or even to our dog, we want them to be captivated by it to act on our ideas. We use stories in business and in everyday life, in formal situations and when passing people in the street. Mastering the art of storytelling allows us to reach the hearts and minds of the people we come into contact with. When we tell our story it is about selling the story.

This is so important for every goal we want to reach in life that I want to dedicate this section to the art of telling and selling an idea and ultimately getting support, buy-in and followers.

There are three important things to keep in mind when selling and telling a story. Ideally embrace all three of them:

1 *Shoot for the heart,* because people remember when they are emotionally connected with your story.
2 *Capture the mind,* which is the rational part of the brain, and the rational part of your audience.
3 *Make your audience smile,* because humour releases energy, can facilitate social interactions and contributes to higher subjective wellbeing.

Tintin Snack: the archetype of energising. Steve Ballmer, former CEO of Microsoft, embodies energising. He had so much love for the company that everyone could see his energy in everything he said and did.

Every year Microsoft people from around the world get together for an inspirational global business summit, and of course to have some fun. This global summit gives them enough energy for the rest of the year. They go back to work fully loaded about the company, who they are, the why and what and with an outlook on the future. For the twenty-two years I worked at Microsoft, I was fortunate enough not to miss a single one. Ballmer is one of the smartest people I've ever met, he's passionate, he has unbelievable energy, he's an amazing storyteller and uses humour. An authentic person who embodies energising, shooting for the heart and the mind with humour.

However, research has shown that fear of public speaking, also known as speech anxiety or glossophobia, is the greatest fear that people have, even greater than that of spiders, disease and death itself. Some people are so scared they start sweating, they can't sleep, they don't smile when they're on stage, or if they do it's a Snoopy smile, pretending to be happy. If someone is scared and doesn't smile genuinely, people will feel their fear.

Public speaking doesn't just mean to a room of more than fifty people. In a sense *public* speaking is speaking with more than one person.

'The biggest fear is public speaking, with 15% of Americans experiencing a dramatic fear of it,' said Dr Michael Telch of the Laboratory for the Study of Anxiety Disorders (LSAD) in the Department of Psychology at The University of Texas at Austin.

Tintin Snack: field journalism. During my life at Microsoft I learned from Bob Béjan, former Advertising and Online Lead for Microsoft US and today Global GM of Communications, what field journalism and storytelling means. When presenting, he uses beautiful words. Like a poet on steroids, he orchestrates his story in big public presentations, and being a singer he uses music to bring his story to life. He shoots for the heart, captures the mind and makes people smile.

If you are one of the many who fears public speaking, follow my five rules to overcome your fears, as communication is the ultimate toolkit for taking people with you on the digital journey, convincing them, inviting them to join the adventure and making them dream. Very few master all of the below, but improving on each of them will make your life much easier.

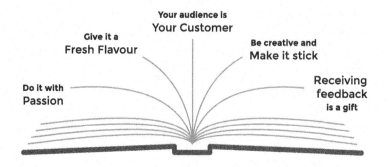

Communicating your ideas is the currency of today to evolve your brand. If you improve your storytelling skills, you will increase the value of yourself and the business you represent.

Carmine Gallo, Keynote speaker, author of The Storyteller's Secret

1. Do it with passion. Life without passion is no life. This is where we need to touch the heart. In order to connect with other people's hearts, we have to be vulnerable, show that we are human beings so the audience can relate to us. To feel like we're connecting with them, every single individual needs to see how real we are. They want to know whether we are a big ego or whether there is vulnerability.

Here are some hints for touching the audience's heart:

- Sparkle on stage. Make sure your eyes sparkle, engage with the audience so that they feel inspired and connected. Very good speakers interact with the audience, asking questions, engaging, even walking through the audience
- Remain in attendance. No one wants to listen to an automaton. If the audience feels you're reciting your speech from memory, they will feel like a robot is talking. They will not feel any authenticity
- Master your talk. It's much easier to show your passion during the presentation when you have mastered it. Then you can make your passion contagious so people feel elevated from their chairs and want to join you
- Be persuasive. Making your audience dream is very important, and using 'what if?' questions will touch their emotions and help you to persuade them
- Show your passion to express your talent. Tell your story with passion and conviction. A good story is 65% emotions and feeling.

2. Bring something fresh. Surprise your audience with something they didn't expect. Your mission is to inform, educate, inspire and give people a new way to look at the world in which they live. Many people talk about the same subject, but the way you relate to the audience, showing a different point of view or a different way of looking at a problem, will make the topic fresh.

You need to grasp attention, and to get the audience's attention you have to do something new and unexpected. Surprise them. It is the age of serendipity, after all.

> **Tintin Snack: surprise people.** Bill Gates is a great speaker, but he didn't always express emotions easily. He was seen as very smart, but not many people realised he has a great sense of humour.
>
> One of the things he's passionate about, and hopes to cure with the Bill and Melinda Gates Foundation, is malaria. At the end of one of his TED speeches, he surprised the audience completely. He had a small glass box in the middle of the stage, and he explained that the mosquito is the most dangerous insect in the world. He then said, 'I've brought some mosquitoes with me', opened the box and the mosquitoes flew into the audience of 700 people. 'It should not only be the poor who get bitten by mosquitoes. The rich should also get exposure. By the way, those mosquitoes are harmless.'

Not every speech has to have a single jaw dropping 'oh shit!' moment, but having a few surprises and creative ideas that people didn't expect is a great move. A speech should express all the emotions like joy, fear, shock and surprise as the brain has a kind of a save button for these things. People will always remember the small pieces that were fresh ways of looking at the world.

Tintin Snack: music moves. A great way to get a jaw dropping moment is with short music videos. When you show a great video of half a minute and watch the audience, you will see the people melt while the video's playing. They smile because they can relate to the video. Often when you end with music, it's beautiful too.

For example, Steve Ballmer mastered the art of adding music to his talks. At the end of his sessions at Microsoft, he talked during the song he wanted to make his point. That's the cherry on the cake. It's the climax.

3. Remember your audience is your customer. You are here for the audience. You need to think of your audience as your friends, students, managers or family, whether it's a huddle of professors, a bunch of kids or a posse of investors who want to invest in your business. They are all in one, and you want to reach each of them. Tailor your message to them. Think about what they want to hear.

Make sure you're talking for the audience. If you're talking to kids, adapt your story. Make it simple for them to understand.

The heart of your presentation is the customer who might buy your product or your ideas. Have empathy or a connection with the audience, feel where the audience is. If people start looking at their mobile phones and frowning, or there's a murmur at the back, maybe take a pause, make a joke, ask a question, or be a little bit provocative.

Be honest to build fans, and make sure that when you present to your audience, your values come across. If you're presenting your company, you present the values of the company. Encourage people to want more. At the end of the presentation, gauge the sound of the applause, note how many people come to you or ask to be friends on LinkedIn, count the number of tweets. This is your feedback on how well you have engaged with your audience.

4. Make it stick. Be creative in how you present and visualise your ideas. You need to deliver a great experience and avoid sleeping audiences by making the message stick. There are five ways to make it stick.

Practise, practise, practise. I didn't believe this at first, but I always practise now even if it's limited. Practise in front of a mirror, or your family and friends, but make sure you practise. Be careful that your practice doesn't robotise your presentation. Try not to have every word fixed in your head. Have notes, a few bullet points to remind you what you want to say. Some people might need more, but don't overdo it.

Some people do it differently. Steve Jobs, for the big annual events around September in Silicon Valley, would practise for four full days. Why? The final moment, always ending with 'One more thing', was worth hundreds of millions of marketing dollars as it would go viral. Steve Jobs knew the strength of communication. This perfectionism and the four days of practice were so valuable.

Humour. It's not about telling a joke, unless of course you are a comedian. Use funny anecdotes, especially about kids, family and friends, that people can relate to, because we're all human beings. Using humour will make you likeable, and people will be more open to doing business with you if they like you. Lower your defences, and when the audience smiles, it lowers its defences too. Even if you can't be funny, try a little self-deprecating humour. Laugh at yourself, but make sure you remain authentic.

Deliver the experience. You have to master your stage presence. The whole picture has to be one: the way you sound, the way you move, your clothes. Have your own style that works for you and your audience, formal or informal. Storytelling is how you present, how you come on stage, how you move around on stage, so be dynamic, express yourself with your body language. Your presentation needs to be visual, but limit text on the slides. The titles of the slides are the most important, then a single image can convey your idea beautifully and elegantly.

How do you make your story delicious and beautiful? If you want to enlist people, you need to make things beautiful, and you do that by visualisation.

> **Tintin Snack: titles tell the story.** The president of the media agenda Omnicom Media Group EMEA, Nikki Mendonça, is a master in pitching. She told me years ago that when she gets a brief or a pitch from a client, she only looks at the titles of the slides. If you remove the rest of the text from any slide, the titles have to tell the story.

Avoid sleeping audiences. If you have a pitch, a presentation or a story that takes an hour or two, make sure every ten to fifteen minutes, you reengage. Do a demonstration or show a video, tell a new story or joke. Then at the end, for a maximum of five minutes, share the key take-aways and the three reasons why the audience should support your idea.

Tintin Snack: don't make your audience sleepy! A TED Talk is on average eighteen minutes long, because eighteen minutes is apparently the attention span a person has without falling asleep or being distracted by something else. That's why you need to keep reengaging if you have a longer story.

Tonality and pacing matters. There's some great support on the web about the tone you use, the pauses you make. When you tell a joke, give the audience time to laugh. Don't just go on, pause. Find your timings. Your voice shouldn't be a monotone. Practise a lot and model good speakers.

> **Tintin Snack: start-up pitching.** If you're a start-up, on average you are probably pitching with ten others to sell your idea. Everyone talks about the start-up market dynamics: team and customers, problems and product, competition, timing and finance. The people who've listened to nine other start-ups are probably drifting off to sleep by the time they listen to yours.
>
> So, how do you stand out? Try to do all the things we've already looked at – add humour, capture hearts and minds, project your passion. But timing is super critical as often you only get five to eight minutes, so manage your time carefully. If you only have five minutes, don't take ten minutes. People appreciate you valuing their time.

5. Feedback is a gift. There are three great opportunities for getting feedback – in the rehearsal stage, during your speech and afterwards. You receive feedback through the emotions and the laughs you get from the audience while you are presenting, you get feedback when you practise and you have feedback afterwards.

The person who sets the boundaries for feedback is the one who asks for the feedback. For example, after the session you may ask someone how the presentation went, but as he or she responds your face changes. He or she sees that you don't like their feedback and stops giving it. You have to be open and receptive. This is valid for all feedback in all types of circumstances.

Tintin Snack: cultural differences. Some cultures are less emotional than others. For example, people are very polite in some countries and nod along, while in other countries they are more demonstrative.

In Japan, an English speaker will need a translator. Then when the speaker asks a question, they are so respectful, so polite and scared they don't respond. Often I found when I asked silent audiences if they had any questions during a workshop, the room would go silent. I quickly learned that I needed to pause. Ask a question and let the silence do its work. People hate silence. After a minute and forty very long seconds, they would start asking questions, and once the first question had been asked, everyone joined in. They felt more comfortable once the ice was broken.

When asking for feedback, you can be specific – ask about the physical aspects, the sound, tonality, your clothing, movement, how you held the microphone. You can ask for feedback on the content, the structure. Was there something fresh? Ask for feedback on how the audience felt – did you shoot for their hearts? Did they have an emotional connection to your story? Did you emotionally connect with them? You can ask if your message stuck. Can they tell you what the key message was? What did they remember?

During your presentation look at the audience's eyes. Are people looking in your direction? Are they laughing in the right places? Are people engaged in a sense? Are they talking among themselves or are they responding to your questions?

Tintin Snack: a speech that has it all – telling and selling in action. Steve Jobs in his famous Stanford commencement speech in 2006 got everything just right. He never went to university, and he started by saying the closest he got to a graduation ceremony was there and then on stage – self-deprecating humour. Then he shared the three stories of his life. Nothing more, nothing less. He talked for fifteen minutes about people finding what they love, what they want to do with their life. He advised the audience to follow their heart and intuition, keep looking, not to settle.

Then he said, 'If this was my last day alive, would I do what I did today?'

He was unbelievably fresh. He made that statement based on his own authenticity, had some humour at the beginning, connected with hearts and minds and left people smiling. He showed he was a human, just like you and me.

To summarise, to be a great storyteller, selling and telling your story, you have to capture the mind, shoot for the heart and make people smile. This is the healthy, mature story seller and teller.

Having a digital strategy will soon look as ridiculous as having an electricity strategy.

Kay Boycott, CEO, Asthma UK

Start-ups and incumbents – the best of both worlds. We're not there yet, but soon digital will be part of the core DNA of any company.

Established companies have a lot of assets that start-ups don't, and vice versa. When big companies try to mimic start-ups or foster the mindset of start-ups, they need to remember they have something that most start-ups don't – customers. They also have an organisation, people, value in their brand, supporters, loyalty, investors, stakeholders, shareholders and boards. There's an ecosystem. What the incumbents don't have is the fluidity, flexibility, speed and agility that start-ups have, and they might lack the talent and the right digital mindset.

STARTUP PHASES

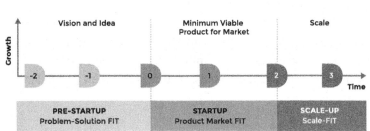

Source http://www.startoutup.com/flag/, Olivier Van Duüren

There are three main stages start-ups go through:

1 Pre-start-up stage: they have a vision, an idea. They conceptualise something, thinking about the customer and how they will solve customers' problems. The most difficult thing to answer is what problems they are trying to solve and for whom. This is the problem-solution FIT stage
2 Start-up stage: they start showing commitment, have customer validation that they have a market valuable product (MVP) – a product-market FIT. They will do some testing, get feedback from clients, iterate the process. Many start-ups reside quite a while in this phase because moving on, scaling and especially profitably, is far more difficult. This is the product-market FIT stage
3 Scale-up: they're establishing growth, trying to get to profitable cash flow, scaling. They are creating bigger customer bases and aim to come close to unicorn. This is the scale-FIT stage.

Each stage has unique elements. Most start-ups will get money in phases one and two, and in the US there's a good balance between funding for the three phases. In Europe, however, most funding goes to phases one and two, making it very hard when start-ups need to scale because then they need more money, bigger numbers.

At the scale up and grow stage is where only one in ten, just 10%, succeed on average. You could stay on the start-up summits for lifelong constant learning in this amazing start-up ecosystem, but don't be blinded. At some point you'll need to go from start-up to scale-up. There's only one judge of when this time comes – it's not the coach or mentor, your peers, family, friends, partner, child. The only judge is the customer.

To scale up and grow you will need to find funding. If you don't find it in your country, go abroad as money has no frontiers; it is 'pan-world', as Fred Destin from Accel Partners says. At this stage you'll need a strong CEO or manager, often not the person who founded the company. This is where established companies could help to find people with track records in building long lasting businesses.

In the new world it might not just be the big fish eating the small fish, but the fast, smaller fish eating the slow fish. An example is start-up EVA Automation, a young start-up without revenue but with forty employees. Led by Gideon Yu, a Silicon Valley veteran, EVA Automation bought the thirty-year-old audio system builder Bowers & Wilkins (B&W), with 1,100 employees and a $120 million turnover. Alternatively, we might see a slow, big fish eating a small digital fish to accelerate its own digital transformation, or bigger fish eating younger fish, like Microsoft's recent acquisition of LinkedIn.

Which type of fish are you?

Many companies are trying to figure out how to get the start-up mentality. McKinsey[136] believes we can do that through the following: organisational pivots (change the organisation), reverse takeover (ring fencing digital operations), spin-off (slice the business up) or piggyback on other people's ideas (partnerships). Many other interesting approaches are on the market and we need to find what fits best. Try, fail, learn, and try again.

In order to grow in the past, to reach international markets, many built structures, organisation, regional headquarters, layer after layer of reporting and scorecards, and hierarchies, resulting in frustrated employees and killed creativity. Leaders of today will need to change the way they are organised. The challenge for companies that have lost their creativity and fluidity is to embrace change and discover the start-up mentality. People are attracted by start-ups because of the freedom of creativity.

Complexity kills 10% of profits every year. An estimated $237 billion annually in just the top 200 companies.

Jonathan Becher, Chief Digital Officer SAP

Imagine if you could bring the best of both start-ups and incumbents and fuse them, removing the organisational burden, noise and hierarchies. Imagine unleashing creativity for bigger organisations. Imagine decentralising smaller teams or giving them independence and freedom to innovate.

To get the mindset of the start-ups, we need to simplify structures, make collaboration centre stage, remove individuals who do not collaborate, break down boundaries, and adjust incentive, pay and bonus plans to foster collaboration across boundaries, across organisations. And if that doesn't help, we need to determine our worst nightmare then build a team and business to solve it.

Trend spotting, a geeks' and a kids' board. How do we make sure we continue to see what is out there? How can this be part of the way we operate?

Kids see the world through a different lens. They are fresh, creative, unbounded, unconfined, without preconceived ideas. There's a wonderful video from Microsoft that helps people to reconnect with their inner child. Go to the website resources section for the link to Kids Video. 'We wanted to see the future, so we asked people with the boldest vision. You know, kids. In summary, with a little imagination everything is possible.'

In the video, kids between the ages of six and ten are asked how they see the future. Their innocence is disarming even for the most jaded business person, but that's not the most important thing to take away. These kids, with their unlimited view of the world, their unhindered expectations of the future, were able to predict the Google car. They could imagine the IoT where everything is connected.

Tintin Snack: Kids are the digital makers – digital natives born with digital literally at their fingertips – and they see the world very differently. They have a different reference framework. My view, born in 1968, was playing with Action Man, watching a couple of TV channels, and my first computers were a Spectrum Texas, a Commodore 64, an Apple II C and an Apricot.

One of the tricks for thinking about the possibilities of the world is not to use our own reference framework. Consider having a 'kids' board' for your company to challenge your ways of thinking. Get kids to give their opinions about what you're doing and what you could do as they are very creative.

Tintin Snack: learning from kids. I admit I'm a techno-design geek. My home has a lot of the newest gadgets and design innovations, with screens and technology in every room. A couple of years ago, my youngest nephew visited and I introduced him to Kinect, the natural body scanning system you can talk to. He was about five years old and was already playing with iPads and gadgets, so I taught him how to talk to the Xbox and he started playing with Kinectimals, a beautiful game. At some point he wanted to change the game, so he went up to the big screen and started swiping across it, because that's how he'd interacted with technology so far.

Now, remember I admitted that I'm into new technology. At the time we had a fridge with a limited computer that could do a few interesting thing. When we had dinner that evening, my nephew walked up to the fridge and started talking to it. He had already learned that you can talk to technology.

Kids are so adaptive. They see opportunities, they can transpose things they've learned in digital to the rest of their world. A *kids' board* would think with a different reference framework. Go out today and find yourself some youngsters to help you imagine the future of your business. Some countries even have kids' parliaments that come together once in a while to mirror government and discuss things that matter to kids.

You might also envision a *geeks' board*.[137] MIT has found that digitally adept companies are 26% more profitable than their competitors. However, a 2015 study showed that many boards lacked understanding on how disruptive digital is to a business, or how cybersecurity and digital transformation can steer changes in strategy, decision making and success or failure of a company. At the board level, there is clearly a need for geeks: directors or strong individuals who can put technology to use, who see and can energise to determine the way forward. And this should not only be outsourced to external management consultants or start-ups as digital DNA needs to be at the core of your company. The time is here to act, don't wait. Your internal or external talent pool is limited and waiting to be recruited. So if you don't have any geeks in the company, start hiring some.

Although I loved working on technology – I've always been a computer geek at heart – my professors encouraged me to get a real-world job working with customers.

Marc Benioff, CEO Salesforce.com

Consider installing *a strategic trend watching* and fact finding board at the heart of your company, their objectives being to identify key digital transformation trends in your and other industries and look out for new entrants. They will monitor what the market is saying about you, what your customers are saying, look for competitive trends to inform strategy, digital monetisation opportunities and recommended plans, and determine the conditions to incubate ideas with the right mindset.

Key objectives for your trend watching and fact finding board:

- Act as a trend beacon across groups, independent of hierarchy, to see and advise on key digital transformation trends (consumer, socio-economic), competitive trends, their implications and changes in the digital landscape
- Determine future growth opportunities based on market trends and where the industry demand is going, advise on ways to differentiate, help with defence-offence and/or game changing parts for the whole business
- Identify winning strategies with customers, speed them across locations and best practices, and incubate ideas.

And finally, another option could be to initiate a disruption board. Even if some people might not like the word disruption, it makes it clear what the board's purpose is. Or if you want to be more positive, you could call it an energy board, especially if you feel you need more energy to take the right actions in the Dualarity.

Cracking The Dualarity Code

The companies and people who enjoy the best outcomes are those who can easily live in the Dualarity. They are able to see what needs to be done and have the energy to do it, put systems in place and develop mature companies that perform. They are also able to keep their eyes open to change, see what's happening around them, follow the changes and keep the energy level high – they are able to transform and stay healthy. They understand they need to transform as a person before they can transform their business, can only lead others if they lead themselves first. They are key people of influence and action.

They have balance in the Dualarity.

How do we and our businesses develop the ability to balance in the Dualarity comfortably? How do we keep our energy high and our ability to see what's happening effective? Successful Dualarity heroes have the following characteristics:

- They know their why and what. They have people as their soul, digital as their oxygen and customers at the heart of what they do
- They have engines and appetite for seeing the changes, keeping ahead and sharing their learning. They remain curious and want to learn
- They commit to nurturing, developing, expanding their knowledge. They care about the health of themselves and their workforce to keep the energy levels high
- They map people, products and their business on the Dualarity Quadrant so they know where they are
- They apply the Dualarity principles and toolbox to energise themselves, their loved ones and their businesses
- They transform themselves before they transform others.

The AHA moments
How people realise what to do in life

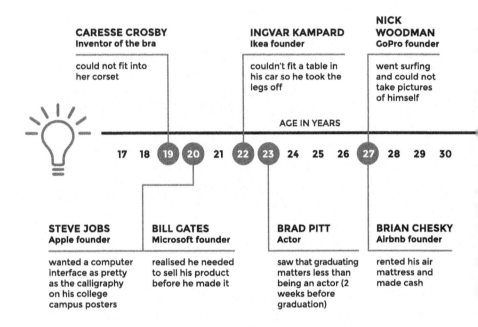

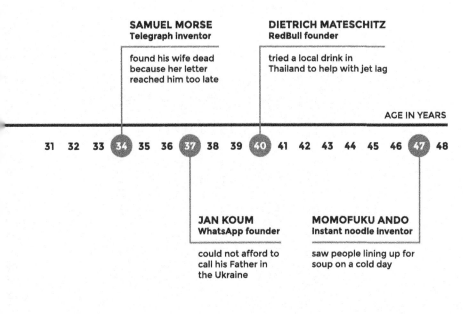

SAMUEL MORSE
Telegraph inventor

found his wife dead
because her letter
reached him too late

DIETRICH MATESCHITZ
RedBull founder

tried a local drink in
Thailand to help with jet lag

AGE IN YEARS

31   32   33   34   35   36   37   38   39   40   41   42   43   44   45   46   47   48

JAN KOUM
WhatsApp founder

could not afford to
call his Father in
the Ukraine

MOMOFUKU ANDO
Instant noodle inventor

saw people lining up for
soup on a cold day

Source Funders and Founders

Tintin Snack: famous aha moments

This infographic from Funders and Founders[138] shows aha moments when people realised what to do with their lives. Bill Gates, Microsoft, realised that he needed to sell his product before he made it and that's what he did. Brad Pitt, the actor, realised that for him graduating mattered less than being an actor two weeks before graduation. Steve Jobs wanted a computer interface as pretty as the calligraphy of his college campus posters.

So what is your aha moment?

Where do you fit in the Dualarity?

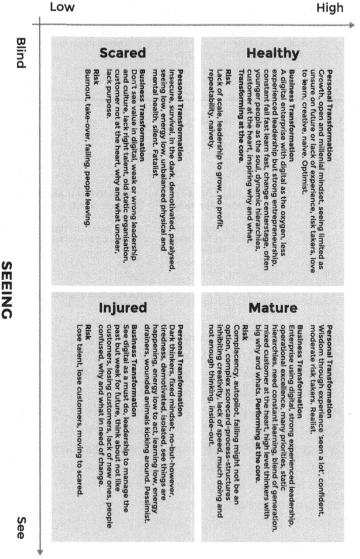

ENERGISING

Low   High

Blind

SEEING

See

Scared

Personal Transformation
Insecure, survival, in the dark, demotivated, paralysed, seeing low, energy low, unbalanced physical and mental health, silent. Fatalist.

Business Transformation
Don't see value in digital, weak or wrong leadership and culture, lack right talent, old static organisation, customer not at the heart, why and what unclear, lack purpose.

Risk
Burnout, take-over, failing, people leaving.

Healthy

Personal Transformation
Growth, open and millenial mindset, seeing limited as unsure on future or lack of experience, risk takers, love to learn, creative, naïve. Optimist.

Business Transformation
A digital enterprise with digital as the oxygen, less experienced leadership but strong entrepreneurship, constant fail fast learn fast, change centerstage, often younger people as the soul, dynamic hierarchies, customer at the heart, inspiring why and what. Transforming at the core.

Risk
Lack of scale, leadership to grow, no profit, repeatability, naïvety.

Injured

Personal Transformation
Dark thinkers, fixed mindset, no-but-however, tiredness, demotivated, isolated, see things are happening, energy low to act, learning low, energy drainers, wounded animals kicking around. Pessimist.

Business Transformation
See digital as a must do, leadership to manage the past but weak for future, think about not like customers, losing customers, lack of new ones, people confused, why and what in need of change.

Risk
Lose talent, lose customers, moving to scared.

Mature

Personal Transformation
Wisdom through experience 'seen a lot', confident, moderate risk takers. Realist.

Business Transformation
Enterprise using digital, strong experienced leadership, operational excellence, many priorities, static hierarchies, need constant learning, blend of generation, mixed customer at the heart, high level thinkers with big why and whats. Performing at the core.

Risk
Complacency, autopilot, failing might not be an option, complex scorecard-process-structures inhibiting creativity, lack of speed, much doing and not enough thinking, inside-out.

Finding out where you and your business sit in the Dualarity Quadrant will help you develop plans and strategies for moving forwards. Remember the Dualarity Quadrant isn't a place where you are static; you are able to move from quadrant to quadrant as you learn and see more and become energised by the future.

The first step is to use the Dualarity fitness test to find your own place in the Dualarity Quadrant, and then to find your company's place. Go ahead and take the fitness test now.

Here are some insights of how you can move from one place to another, from one quadrant to another.

Coaching in the quadrants

Moving out of the scared quadrant. People and businesses in this quadrant are searching for certainty, security, energy and seeing. If you find yourself or your business in the scared quadrant, this is what you can do:

1. Personal transformation.

- Accept where you are now, acknowledge it's not a great place to be, decide you want to change. You need to find peace of mind
- Communicate about your state, your condition. Be open and transparent so people understand and will reach out to you. In your personal life, communicate with friends and professionals who can help you. In business, communicate with colleagues, across departments, look outside your own environment and ask for help from professionals, consultants, peers in the industry and mentors
- Take action, and take care of your own physical and mental health (the golden triangle). Start on a personal level, do sports, find fun things to do with friends. Then go on courses, learn, get ahead of the curve, get inspiration, learn to see

again, move. Plan thinking and creative moments to determine the actions you could take. Work with internal and external experts and people willing to join the action plan. And as face to face connections are the most important aspects of being healthy and happy, increase the frequency of them. Increase your resilience so you can be shielded from falling back into the scared quadrant.

2. Business transformation.

- Leverage digital to function as oxygen for your organisation. Do it step by step by step, and make sure you find support in your digital seeing so you know what is happening around you
- Embrace the feedback of your customers and see how you can redefine their experience. Ask them to be involved so you put them at the heart of your business. If you have loyal customers, they will want to help you
- Hire talent, acquire a smaller tech company or work with external consultants. Hire new leadership if needed and have the younger talent drive parts of the transformation
- Reset your why and what completely
- Look for partnerships, alliances or someone who might be willing to acquire your business, but you'll need to do some of the above first if you want to increase your value and chances of success.

> The more injuries you get, the smarter you get.
> **Mikhail Baryshnikov, Ballet Dancer**

Recovering from injury. The long tail of injured people and companies will seek people like themselves and unite around common enemies, wallowing in dark thinking and not seeing the light at the end of the tunnel. They become part of the 'no, but, however' community. Seeking people with similar states of mind risks creating a constrained tunnel vision, so how do they recover from injury? If you're a business or individual stuck in this quadrant, what do you need to do?

1. Personal transformation.

- Accept where you are now, acknowledge it's not a great place to be, decide you want to change
- Heal and recover – look for opportunities to align with energised people and organisations. Look outside your own environment and ask for help from professionals, consultants and mentors. Look for people who are opposites of you, the positive tribes in the organisation or friends. Join them to recover. Do reverse mentoring where possible
- Act – take care of your own physical and mental injuries first. Recruit, retrain and retain high energy Dualarity heroes. Allow them to lead the journey for a while. Revive where you can and heal the wounds.

2. Business transformation.

- Try to become a digital enterprise instead of an enterprise using some digital because you have no choice. Think about your processes, business models and operations and what you do with digital
- Hire some strong digital leadership to partner with your experienced leaders. Hire a digital officer to start with or find one internally. Hire a customer experience or user design strategy leader so you think about your customers
- Rehire your people and hire some new talent. Make small tech acquisitions if needed. Organise hackathons with employees, partners and customers so you re-energise the organisation
- Redefine the why, who, how and what. Communicate a lot and practise field journalism.

Move out of your comfort zone. You can only grow if you are willing to feel awkward and uncomfortable when you try something new.

Brian Tracy

Staying healthy balanced with mature. If you feel you, or your business, are in the healthy quadrant, with high energy but limited seeing, how can you ensure you don't get injured? How can you scale up or land in the mature quadrant?

1. Personal transformation.

- Learn – this is what you're great at, learning with an open mindset. Communicate with colleagues, across departments, look outside your own environment and ask for advice from professionals, consultants and mentors to grow further. If you are a start-up then learn from the incumbents as they have experience. Start spotting trends and find people who have seen a lot and have mastered being healthy and mature. Find the Dualarity heroes. Continue to fail fast but learn fast. Keep your eyes open and be an optimistic realist
- Accept – scaling, maturing, 'growing up' are normal parts of life. Realise that maturing is only a state and you can bounce back into the healthy quadrant whenever you want and need to. This bouncing back is the best place to be – the Dualarity pendulum.
- Act – scale your business, get funding, grow.

2. Business transformation.

- Hire a business leader who is experienced in growing businesses as a partner to the more entrepreneurial leader. Complement the younger talent with more experience without losing the culture of your company

- Grow your customer base by finding repeatable customer journeys and asking your customers to join your evolution
- Find new monetisable streams and test them out. Find new funding arenas and keep on investing any profit in new innovative solutions
- Keep looking at your why and what and see where you are.

Avoiding complacency as you mature. Maturity comes when a person or business stops making excuses and starts making things happen; when the business has scaled and outgrown the start-up phase.

However, with maturity can come complacency as people believe they have the solution, are able to see what's happening, know everything, are doing well and have the energy to do even more. The biggest risk is for people to be working on autopilot, trying to excel in everything and measure everything they do with a complex process, scorecard, reporting system, organisation chart and templates so they can squeeze even more and keep hold of central control and power. This brings the danger of becoming an inside-out company with too many priorities, so people barely have time to meet customers or be creative and entrepreneurial again. They are being asked to execute while being inspected, unable to question or open their mindset any more.

Take care of your personal and business transformation, and perform while transforming.

1. Personal transformation.

- Try to reinvent yourself and surround yourself with new and younger talent. Have an open mindset and challenge your own reference framework of thinking. Ask your family, friends and colleagues how you are doing and see feedback as a gift. Ask for a 360-degree review at work and listen to your customers.

Don't try to show you have answers to everything, but ask open questions and answer questions with 'I don't know, but let's find out'

- Find a new inspiring personal goal or sparkle so you don't get stuck in your own *Groundhog Day* movie Breakdown the routines and automatism.
- Don't be blinded or fooled by your current personal success as everything has a timestamp on it. See and understand what is happening around you
- Don't blame the system as you are part of the system. You can find the coalition of the willing so you are part of the change needed to innovate and be fresh again. Fight complex systems, procedures and reports that keep you away from thinking, creating and your customers
- Find a new charter if needed, outside or inside the company, so you learn new things and have a new set of eyes.

2. Business transformation.

- Avoid complacency – make sure you stay alert. Think about your worst nightmare and build a business around it, like Facebook has done. Think about what-if scenarios and stay creative. Keep your eyes wide-open, and don't say, 'I know'. Don't slow down. You might be dominating an area, but if you're too inward looking, customers will run to new entrants in your market
- Reinvent or reimagine yourself and parts of your business over and over. Perform and transform and avoid getting stuck in the quarter by quarter delivery. Think about yesterday, today, tomorrow and the day after tomorrow at the same time. Make room for innovation and unleash creativity. Allow some level of chaos and don't try to reach operational excellence in everything you do. (See the Geographic clusters of the Dualarity genius part to get more insights on this). Find your new sparkle so the fire doesn't disappear

- Put the customer back at the heart of the company by reducing all internal must-dos and non-value processes and reporting. Give people time to be with customers
- Instil a culture of performing while transforming (see 'transformational leadership and cultural attributes' in the 'Dualarity Toolbox' section).
- Enhance your skills of seeing the next big thing and energising your people to find new areas of growth and new markets to enter. Infuse entrepreneurship, Millennial and start-up mindsets in the company. Re-hire some of your current employees and hire some new talent in all levels of the organisation. Inspiring your teams is your new mission in life
- Give your organisation sparkles so you don't just become an operational machine. Change parts of your leadership and simplify your organisation by removing layers and entities that don't make sense at all.

Give room to the heart, the soul and the body of your company so you can remain healthy while being mature. Ride the waves of the Dualarity pendulum.

Tintin Snack: today, tomorrow and the day after tomorrow. During one of the talks I attended, Peter Hinssen, serial entrepreneur and radical innovation consultant, explained that organisations should balance working on today, tomorrow and the day after tomorrow. He explained the energy, resources and time spend could be split into 70% today, 20% tomorrow and 10% day after tomorrow. Peter then explained that one day after his presentation, a senior executive came to him and said he'd missed something critical.

'There is something before that, something before today: the shit of yesterday, which needs to be cleaned out every day.' In other words, if you're not careful, you end-up spending 90% of your day on cleaning up yesterday and today and there's less than 10% left for tomorrow and the day after tomorrow.

Summary Energising

Given the magnitude of the changes in the world and the scarcity of skills and capabilities in the smart interconnected products and services for home and work, many organisations will need to pursue hybrid strategies and approaches. Leverage the Dualarity principles and toolbox to help you move forward into the Dualarity.

See the world as it is, what it will become, and energise yourself to perform while you transform. The Dualarity at its best.

> Seeing is time-based, energising yourself is timeless!
>
> **Olivier Van Duüren**

The Dualarity Fitness Test

The Dualarity
Fitness Test

We went from seeing what is happening in the world of accelerated change to energising by following the principles and tools of the Dualarity Toolbox to go through personal and business transformation and learn how to inspire and lead others. We have to make sure our leadership and organisation are behind us. We need the CEO, or even better the whole board, really backing the transformation and creating the right conditions to succeed.

The next steps will be to go through the Dualarity fitness tests:

1   Test your personal digital transformation
2   Test your business digital transformation.

Map yourself so you can transform. In order to transform your business, you must first transform yourself. The best way to transform yourself is to discover where you are on the Dualarity Quadrant, so answer the questions on the test honestly.

There are more sophisticated ways of scoring, but to keep it easy to measure I've simplified how to test yourself and your business in this book. This fitness test will evolve, so make sure to check www.thedualarity.com where evolved online versions are available.

Personal Dualarity Fitness Test

These first statements are about you. This is a very simple test and only a guide to your current position on the Dualarity Quadrant. Rate each statement 1 to 5 to show which most closely resemble your current thinking, view or position.

Ratings: 1=strongly disagree; 2=disagree; 3=neutral; 4=agree; 5=strongly agree. Think about yourself in the digital transformation as you answer the personal Dualarity readiness statements below:

Plan your life

1   You have a good balance in your wellbeing triangle of sleep, nourishment and exercise
2   You plan enough thinking moments in advance for yourself and your teams
3   You know your sparkle (one or two things that will make you proud) and how to find it.

Constant learning

4   You feel you have the right digital skills. You embrace digital and technology, you are active on social media, buy up to date digital tech and you like to talk about it
5   You spend enough time in digital seeing, trend watching, reading and learning what is happening out there
6   You are part of any reverse mentoring effort
7   You have plenty of great colleagues and find it handy having younger generations around so you can learn from them
8   You try to stay ahead of the curve.

Mature and healthy balance

9   You have a lot of passion and high energy
10 You are able to disrupt and transform yourself and are open to breaking into new fields
11 You see the future most often as a glass half full (optimist)
12 You like people who see a world full of opportunities. You are a 'yes we can' type and like to change things to see them through
13 You love your work. It stretches you, makes you think, and you always learn new things
14 You believe robots and machine learning will not take your job away but will change the way you work, and you know your future will change
15 You live in the moment, not waiting for your pension to enjoy work and life
16 You are a great storyteller and seller
17 You leave your ego at the door
18 You enjoy taking risks
19 You are able to perform and transform.

Add up your total. Max. score = 95 (19 times 5), min. score = 19 (19 times 1).

If you scored 19–38 points you are scared, maybe injured.

If you scored 39–59 points, you're possibly injured.

If you scored over 60, you are healthy or mature. To find out which quadrant is dominating, have a look at the 'Cracking The Dualarity Code' graph.

If you scored over 80, you are close to or already are a Dualarity Hero.

Business Dualarity Fitness Test

These statements are to help you work out where your business falls in the Dualarity Quadrant. Rate them as you did with the personal test.

Put customers at the heart

1 You have frictionless and seamless customer experiences today
2 You are a customer-centric organisation. You think like a customer, you have a user or customer design strategy in place, and customers are involved in designing your offerings
3 You truly understand your customers' needs, wants and behaviours so you can have a more personalised approach
4 Your digital customer feedback, originating from all channels (e.g. social, support, PR), is well integrated in your strategy
5 You have clear customer experience metrics in place and you can track them through real-time data systems.

See people as the soul

6 You know who your Dualarity heroes are – those who are healthy or mature, those who can perform and transform and those who can adapt to new ways of working
7 You have a coalition of the willing in place
8 You feel you have a future-proof organisation ready for the digital transformation
9 Your organisation has talent and enough digital skills in-house to succeed
10 There is enough diversity in place, e.g. a mix of old, young, genders, races, etc.
11 You have a strong employee retention rate with digital retraining and recruitment programmes in place

12 You have the right digital leadership with one of the three critical roles in place: digital officer, design officer or data officer

13 You organise hackathons to blend generations, employees and external parties like start-ups to foster digital ideation

14 Your workplace is adapting new ways of working, leveraging the newest technology so people feel empowered

15 Your operational excellence, scorecards, process reporting and hierarchies are not limiting your creativity and transformation

16 You have rewards and incentives in place for those who transform and continue performing. You reward cross-boundary collaboration

17 Your culture enables people to fail successfully. Failing is allowed as long as people learn quickly

18 Your organisation has an open growth mindset with room for conflict and feedback

19 You have regular meetings with open communication (status, successes and failures) and field journalism in general

20 You have a trend spotting, geeks' or kids' board in place

21 You don't have priorities that prevent you from transforming.

Make digital the oxygen of your company

22 Your digital transformation strategy is supported at the company level and seen as a strategic (oxygen of the company) versus a me-too tactical approach

23 Senior management creates the conditions (people, digital, customer experience, why and what) to succeed in the digital journey, and you have the right digital leadership

24 Your management inspires with action and authenticity in the transformation

25 You have set aside the right budgets that go across all departments. The company is committed to going beyond the traditional 10% innovation budgets

26 You have real-time connected 'source of truth' analytics generating

insights available for your people and the key decision-makers

27 You have a clear privacy and security strategy in place across the organisation and you give your customers the right level of transparency about how you use their data

28 The basic business outcomes and monetisation models are defined for the digital transformation even if they might not be clear due to the speed of the changes (remember fail fast, learn fast)

29 Your digital processes, operations and business model are in line with your digital strategy

30 You have strong digital transformation efforts compared to the market and your direct competitors

31 Your organisation has prioritised the innovation projects (IoT, machine learning, robots, sensors, etc.) you want to implement

32 Your company is doing some targeted acquisitions in the technology space to accelerate its digital transformation.

Your purpose

33 Your leadership has defined a compelling and inspiring purpose (why and what) for your transformation and future success.

Add up your total. Max. score = 165 (33 times 5), min. score = 33 (33 times 1).

If you scored 33–66 points, your business is closer to scared, maybe injured.

If you scored 67–99 points, it's possibly an injured business.

If you scored 100 or more, your business is healthy or mature. To find out which quadrant is dominating, have a look at the 'Cracking The Dualarity Code' graph.

If you scored over 135, your business is close to or already is a Dualarity hero business.

How To Move Forward

The Dualarity

A quadrant diagram with vertical axis labeled ENERGISING (High / Low) and horizontal axis labeled SEEING (Blind / See). The four quadrants are: Healthy (top left), Mature (top right), Scared (bottom left), Injured (bottom right).

SEEING

Remember, where you are on the Dualarity Quadrant is an indicator of a moment in time. If you have found yourself or your business in the scared or injured quadrants you have plenty of opportunities to make changes, improve your vision and energise yourself or your team. Read through the Dualarity principles and toolbox sections for ideas.

If you found yourself or your business in the mature or healthy quadrants, while these are great places to be, don't get complacent! Your goal is to become a Dualarity hero, moving between healthy and mature as you develop and grow. Move your organisation or parts of it between the two.

To go to the next stage, overlay your own map on to the map of your team and business to look for alignment, issues and actions

Summary – Your Path To Becoming
A Dualarity Hero

In the midst of this turmoil we are expected to compete, grow, perform and find happiness. And as we have seen, this transformation is not just about technology, innovation and science. It's about people, culture, behaviours, passion and mindsets. After all, it is still a human business.

However, time is limited. It is the only life ingredient that can't be extended by an app or bot. Use your time on this planet wisely. Every minute counts. Stumbling or losing your way once in a while doesn't mean that you are lost forever. Live your life fully.

What will be your personal change?

Putting my heart, body and soul into this writing process, a mix of my observations of the world and how I see it shaping, fed with facts and my learnings during my transformation as a person and in business, has been an experience for me, a kind of therapy. I've tried to detangle humans and give meaning for people at certain stages in their life and journey. I've acted as a subjective journalist like Tintin, a thoughtful, healthy human leader transforming and performing in The Dualarity. I want to support you in staying healthy and mature as a person and a business, to get you there and to understand where you are today. I hope this book will help you not just to survive, but to thrive in the world of Dualarity.

The power of The Dualarity is going to help you to be a healthy Tintin in your own adventure, with more experience and more energy if you apply some of the practices in this book. We all have it in us, we just need to release it.

I invite you to share with me what you think, what worked and didn't work for you, or what is missing and how The Dualarity can be improved. I look forward to participating in and leveraging your sparkle, your talent and work to accelerate the transformation while performing. Discover your own Dualarity and have fun while doing it. Find the balancing act between mindset and skillset.

If you want to lead others, start by leading yourself. If you want to transform your business, start by transforming yourself. Do it passionately and find your sparkle while doing it. If not, just move on and find something else.

So what will be your personal change and business transformation? What if we were all Dualarity heroes? What would be your personal authenticity in the transformation?

Keep in touch, look out for me and let me know how I can help.

Olivier.
#thedualarity

Acknowledgements

I've had the idea of writing a book for many years; I wanted to share my view of the world and my experiences, and I thought writing one in support of my new business The Dualarity would be an excellent idea. So I started this therapeutic, hard-working and hard-thinking adventure, trying to make it interesting for you, the reader, to understand and maybe re-energise yourself.

There was so much to learn: the process of writing and what it means to write a book that people will want to read. Every single 'free' minute went to writing and researching. Everything I saw, read and heard, I thought about how it would fit in my book. Covering a subject I am so passionate about which is in constant change made it challenging, but so rewarding. Launching my Dualarity book and business made the meaning of being physically present but mentally absent clear for my dear family. That's the 'Dualarity' of writing and starting a business, I guess.

I handpicked several people, both within and outside Microsoft, from different parts of the world, asking them to act as beta-readers and read the first draft version of the manuscript. They were kind enough to read it and offered valuable suggestions. From Microsoft: Bob Béjan, GM Communications Microsoft Global (Washington-Seattle); Michel van der Bel, President Microsoft EMEA; Valerie Beaulieu, GM Small & Medium Business Asia; Erin Raynaud, HR Director SMSG International HQ Paris; Leentje Chavatte, Social Marketing Lead Belux; Tim Nagels, Digital Transformation and CMO Belux; Jean-Claude Sandrap, Program Director European Executive Briefing Centre in Brussels. From the non-Microsoft world: Sven Mastbooms, CEO Kindred; André Pelgrims, change architect and director Taking Wing; Peter Vander Auwera, co-founder Innotribe/SWIFT International; Saskia Schatteman, CEO

Media & Entertainment National Television Belgium; Peter Bell, Senior PM Marketo International UK.

I also want to express special thanks to André Pelgrims, who has been a mentor in many stages of my life. André, founder of Taking Wing which helps companies and individuals find balance and grow, has changed who I am for the better with his wisdom of people. To create the Dualarity Quadrant I took some of my learnings from his view on people and organisations.

I am deeply grateful to Debs Jenkins, my 'booksmith', for being a partner in crime, brainstorming for months; for her wisdom, her advice; and for her countless editing drafts, greatly improving each one of them. During the process she became a real friend, and remains a tough boss when it is needed. It has been a true pleasure working with her.

My appreciation goes to my English publisher Rethink Press, a team of talented and smart people. The Managing Editor Lucy McCarraher and Managing Publisher Joe Gregory worked like Yin and Yang for me, so complementary and so passionate about the art of writing, designing and publishing a book. And I want to thank Joanne Coope from Lococo Creative in the UK for helping me to launch my website, design my logo and for the internal pictures in the book.

In life we all have two kinds of families: the one we are born in and the one that we choose to be part of. I am the luckiest man on earth that Heidi Madou chose to be part of mine. It is no exaggeration to say that I never would have been able to write this book without Heidi, who has enchanted me from the day we met. She has given me life guidance and feedback during the whole process. She is my everything, my light in good and bad days, an unbelievable human being and such an amazing mother to our children.

Both my children Manon and Thomas inspired me and gave me great feedback in this creative process, one I feel they also learned from. They allowed me to steal hours from the early morning till late at night to work on the writing and they encouraged me to continue.

The Author

Strategic thinking, transformation and execution are Olivier Van Duüren's base, which he builds on with a focus on people, change management and inspirational leadership.

During 22 years at Microsoft, Olivier has held a number of senior level positions spanning sales, operations, marketing, innovation and strategy across consumer, online, retail, advertising, publishing and enterprise (B2C-B2B) companies in multinational environments. He started working at Microsoft in 1994 and had Benelux, EMEA and Global roles, from working out of the Paris HQ to global travelling to London, Seattle and New York. Prior to joining Microsoft, he spent three years at Hewlett-Packard and is a Commercial Engineering graduate from the Free University in Brussels (VUB).

During his journey Olivier discovered that for businesses to transform successfully they need to transform themselves first so they can transform others. Lead yourself so you can lead others.

In 2016 he founded The Dualarity and wrote the book to help business leaders to find their sparkle in their own transformation. We want to support you in staying healthy and mature as a person and a business, while understanding where you are today. Trying to detangle humans and give meaning for people being at a certain stage in their life, their journey, is all about a Dualarity of being first human and then worker, performing while transforming in the digital revolution. The Dualarity work with individuals and teams to help them perform while transforming themselves into Dualarity heroes.

An author, trend sensemaker, speaker and executive coach, Olivier is a thought leader on personal and business transformation, and on the impact of the changes around us on our society and industry.

Olivier is a fan of the Belgian character Tintin, who personifies his values: a positive adventurer and reporter who conquers the world with never failing vitality. He recovers from difficult situations, he finds solutions, and he's always learning. Even if Tintin gets injured he bounces back to health; if scared, he takes action. For Tintin, as for Olivier, the reward is the journey itself.

The Dualarity Company

Digital transformation and disruption demands a transformation both on a personal and a business level. The changes that are upon us will alter the face of every industry, business and government, and even more importantly the way our society lives.

The Dualarity will help you gain a 360-degree view of what is happening with digital transformation, trends and innovations, and show you how that maps to individuals, consumers, enterprises, and wider socio-economic implications such as the Fourth Industrial Revolution and the future of work. To help you get energised and cope with the transformation, it will provide energising principles and how-tos. There's even a Dualarity fitness test so you can map yourself and your business on the Dualarity quadrant. The Dualarity tools and the fitness test will help you discover the status of your company and yourself by showing what quadrant you're in and how you can move from one quadrant to another. As companies are composed of individuals, it is important to map yourself in The Dualarity before you map others and your business.

I want to support you in staying healthy and mature as a person and a business, getting there and understanding where you are today. Trying to detangle humans and give meaning for people being at a certain stage in their life, their journey, is all about a Dualarity of being first human and then worker, performing while transforming in the digital revolution.

Learn to fly, ride the waves, take action and transform into a butterfly.

What to expect when you work with The Dualarity
- Strategic advice, coaching and workshops on Performing while Transforming
- Personal and Business Transformation
- Digital Transformation = Customer at the Heart, People as the Soul and Digital as the Oxygen
- Behavioural & Business Strategy
- Keynote Speaking and workshops
- Trend sensemaking Society, Industry and Digital
- Entrepreneurship | Starting-up
- Authoring – first book *The Dualarity, Tap into the Energy of Your Personal and Business transformation*
- Scope: International

Visit www.thedualairity.com to:
- Stay up to date on The Dualarity
- Register for the monthly newsletter
- Sign up for seeing and energising tips and ideas
- Take The Dualarity test online
- Book me for an event, a presentation or a workshop
- Order more books.

Connect, share your feedback, ideas and thoughts by using oliviervanduuren@thedualarity.com, Facebook, LinkedIn, the website, or dial my number +32 475 41 32 44.

Dualarity is a Registered Trademark by The Dualarity owned by Olivier Van Duüren.

© Olivier Van Duüren.

Select Bibliography

Brian Solis, *What's The Future Of Business*

Carol S. Pearson, *Awakening The Heroes Within: Twelve archetypes to help us find ourselves and transform our world*

Ray Kurzweil, *The Singularity Is Near*

Simon O. Sinek, *Start With Why: How great leaders inspire everyone to take action (2009)*

Jeff Howe, *The Rise of Crowdsourcing*

Richard Dobbs, James Manyika, Jonathan Woetzel, *No ordinary Disruption*

Klaus Schwab, *The fourth Industrial Revolution*

Carl Frey and Michael Osbourne, *The Future of Employment: How susceptible are jobs to computerisation? and Technology At Work v2.0: The future is not what it used to be*

Martin Ford, *The Rise Of The Robots, Technology and the threat of a jobless future*

Liz Wiseman, *Rookie Smarts: Why learning beats knowing in the new game of work*

Otto Charmer, Katrin Kaufer, *Leading from the Emerging future: from ego-system to eco-system economies*

Erica Ariel Fox, *Winning From Within*

Benjamin Zander, *The Art of Possibility*

Arianna Huffington, *The Sleep Revolution: transforming your life, one night at the time*

Jim Collins, *Good To Great*

Whitney Johnson, *Disrupt Yourself: Putting the power of disruptive innovation to work*

Jonas Ridderstrale and Kjell Anders Nordstrom, *Funky Business – Talent makes capital dance* and *Karaoke Capitalism – Management for mankind*

Salim Ismail, *Exponential Organizations: Why new organizations are ten times better, faster, and cheaper than yours*

Carol Dweck, *Mindset*

Carmine Gallo, *The Storyteller's Secret*

Marshall Goldsmith, *What Got You Here Won't Get You There*

Eric Weiner, *The Geography Of Genius*

Julie Dodd, *The New Reality*

Sir Ken Robinson, *Creative Schools*

Peter Hinssen 'The Network Always Wins'

Max McKeown, *The Strategy Book* and *#Now*

Geert Noels, *Econoshock*

Walter Isaacson, *Steve Jobs*

Jo Caudron and Dado Van Peteghem, *Digital Transformation*

Notes

Introduction

[1] https://en.wikipedia.org/wiki/Superintelligence

[2] Wikipedia – 'In philosophy of mind, dualism is the position that mental phenomena are, in some respects, non-physical, or that the mind and body are not identical.'

[3] http://www.alixpartners.com/en/Publications/AllArticles/tabid/635/articleType/ArticleView/articleId/1820/The-Winners-and-Losers-of-the-Digital-Revolution.aspx#sthash.KUV9kVff.Cn6psbRy.dpbs

The Dualarity Mechanics

[4] http://www.kpcb.com/internet-trends

[5] http://fortune.com/2016/04/18/ibm-revenue-decline-hiring-acquisition/

[6] https://www.linkedin.com/pulse/20141107143151-22992958-j%C3%B8rgen-vig-knudstorp-leading-by-mastering-paradoxical-thinking

[7] http://www.fool.com/investing/general/2015/06/14/5-tech-companies-spending-more-on-rd-than-apple-in.aspx?source=isesitlnk0000001&mrr=1.00

[8] http://www.digitalistmag.com/innovation/2014/10/28/digital-transformation-part-6-examples-of-digital-transformation-done-right-01650489

Seeing Is Understanding

[9] 'The Secret of Enduring Greatness' by Jim Collins, http://www.jimcollins.com/article_topics/articles/secret-of-enduring-greatness.html

10 https://www.linkedin.com/pulse/digital-transformation-put-people-first-tech-follow-gerrie-smits?articleId=6078515672839712768

11 https://www.linkedin.com/pulse/digital-transformation-put-people-first-tech-follow-gerrie-smits?articleId=6078515672839712768

12 http://www.idc.com

13 http://www.ccr-zkr.org/

14 http://www.mckinsey.com/business-functions/mckinsey-digital/our-insights/digital-globalization-the-new-era-of-global-flows

15 http://www.peterhinssen.com/books/the_network_always_wins

16 http://www.mckinsey.com/business-functions/mckinsey-digital/our-insights/digital-globalization-the-new-era-of-global-flows

17 Dave Evans (April 2011): 'The Internet of Things: How the Next Evolution of the Internet Is Changing Everything' (PDF) – http://www.cisco.com/c/dam/en_us/about/ac79/docs/innov/IoT_IBSG_0411FINAL.pdf

18 http://www.mckinsey.com/business-functions/mckinsey-digital/our-insights/digital-globalization-the-new-era-of-global-flows

19 http://www-01.ibm.com/software/in/data/bigdata/ 2012

20 http://omsignal.com/pages/omsignal-bra

21 http://news.microsoft.com/features/connected-cows-help-farms-keep-up-with-the-herd/#sm.0000prepegajddbbw2c1z3wz663bi

22 http://www.amazon.com/b?ie=UTF8&node=10667898011 or watch the video on https://www.youtube.com/watch?v=EHMXXOB6qPA

23 http://futurism.com/smart-city-singapore-going-get-smarter/

24 http://www.smartnation-forbes.com/

25 https://wtvox.com/3d-printing/top-10-implantable-wearables-soon-body/

26 http://www.wired.com/insights/2014/07/data-new-oil-digital-economy/

27 http://www-01.ibm.com/software/in/data/bigdata/ 2012

[28] http://futurism.com/videos/dna-storage-coming-going-revolutionize-way-share-data/

[29] De Tijd – June 6 2015 – Promotie Maken word teen kwestie van data

[30] De Tijd – 11 May 2016 – Slimme App zoekt uw droomjob

[31] http://www.nytimes.com/2014/06/24/technology/microsoft-makes-a-bet-on-quantum-computing-research.html?_r=0

[32] https://www.theguardian.com/technology/2016/jan/02/meet-the-woman-leading-the-race-to-build-the-worlds-first-quantum-computer

[33] http://www.recode.net/2016/4/11/11586022/what-are-bots

[34] http://www.theverge.com/2016/4/6/11378258/taco-bell-ai-bot-slack-crunchwrap-supreme

[35] https://x.ai/

[36] De Tijd June 10 2016 Moeten er nog apps zijn = Comscore, SensorTower and Nomura Research

[37] https://www.youtube.com/watch?v=Y_cqBP08yuA

[38] https://www.youtube.com/watch?v=TnUYcTuZJpM

[39] http://www.wired.com/2016/04/openai-elon-musk-sam-altman-plan-to-set-artificial-intelligence-free

[40] http://www.idc.com/getdoc.jsp?containerId=prUS25329114

[41] https://www.bright.nl/nieuws/enge-gezichtsherkenning-razend-populair-rusland

[42] https://en.wikipedia.org/wiki/Philosophy_of_artificial_intelligence

[43] https://en.wikipedia.org/wiki/Philosophy_of_artificial_intelligence

[44] http://www.theverge.com/2016/4/28/11526436/mark-zuckerberg-facebook-earnings-artificial-intelligence-future

[45] http://www.bbc.com/news/technology-30290540

[46] http://uk.businessinsider.com/microsoft-exec-ai-is-the-most-important-technology-that-anybody-on-the-planet-is-working-on-today-2016-5?r=US&IR=T

[47] http://futurism.com/artificially-intelligent-lawyer-ross-hired-first-official-law-firm/

48 http://techcrunch.com/2016/03/24/microsoft-silences-its-new-a-i-bot-tay-after-twitter-users-teach-it-racism/

49 From https://en.wikipedia.org/wiki/Ten_percent_of_the_brain_myth

50 http://singularityhub.com/2016/05/12/fighting-developing-world-disease-with-ai-robotics-and-biotech/

51 http://futurism.com/videos/hypercells-self-assembling-cells-future/

52 https://www.lily.camera/

53 http://exmachina-movie.com/

54 http://www.forbes.com/sites/janetwburns/2016/01/15/meet-nadine-singapores-new-android-receptionist/#7f4568d12360

55 http://www.telegraph.co.uk/news/2016/03/22/russian-man-to-undergo-worlds-first-full-head-transplant/

56 http://asimo.honda.com/

57 http://futurism.com/images/top-10-humanoid-robots/

58 https://wtvox.com/robotics/top-10-humanoid-robots/

59 http://zorarobotics.be/?lg=en

60 http://www.ifr.org/

61 http://www.engineeringnet.be/belgie/detail_belgie.asp

62 http://www.bbc.com/news/blogs-news-from-elsewhere-36547139

63 https://www.ted.com/talks/raffaello_d_andrea_meet_the_dazzling_flying_machines_of_the_future

64 https://www.microsoft.com/microsoft-hololens/en-us/commercial

65 http://www.pcworld.com/article/3048512/virtual-reality/microsoft-wants-to-holoport-you-into-a-conversation-elsewhere.html

66 http://techcrunch.com/2016/01/23/when-virtual-reality-meets-education/

67 http://www.forbes.com/sites/kbrauer/2015/01/19/top-10-advanced-car-technologies-by-2020

68 http://futurism.com/images/7-benefits-of-driverless-cars/

69 http://www.torontosun.com/2016/04/30/driverless-cars-would-mean-a-lot-more-sex-behind-the-wheel-expert

[70] http://www.fastcompany.com/3056265/start-up-report/this-start-up-lets-users-sell-their-own-shopping-data

[71] http://senseable.mit.edu/

[72] https://en.wikipedia.org/wiki/Crowdsourcing

[73] http://www.crowdsourcing.org/

[74] https://infocus.emc.com/william_schmarzo/nurturing-serendipity-in-the-age-of-data-driven-decisions/

[75] http://techcrunch.com/2014/01/18/amazon-pre-ships/

[76] http://www.people-press.org/2015/09/03/most-millennials-resist-the-millennial-label/

[77] Source: 'Engaging and Cultivating Millennials and Gen Z,' Denison University and Ologie, 12/14

[78] http://www.fastcoexist.com/3045317/what-is-generation-z-and-what-does-it-want

[79] https://www.linkedin.com/pulse/how-millennials-changing-workforce-three-data-trends

[80] http://www.mckinsey.com/mgi/no-ordinary-disruption

[81] http://www.kpcb.com/internet-trends

[82] https://www.weforum.org/reports/global-gender-gap-report-2015

[83] http://www.internal-displacement.org/globalreport2016/

[84] https://www.weforum.org/agenda/2016/04/worlds-fastest-growing-economies

[85] http://www.tijd.be/politiek_economie/internationaal_economie/Cheerleaders_van_globalisering_moeten_luisteren_naar_de_verliezers.9763669-3150.art

[86] http://www.mckinsey.com/business-functions/mckinsey-digital/our-insights/digital-globalization-the-new-era-of-global-flows

[87] http://www.mckinsey.com/business-functions/mckinsey-digital/our-insights/digital-globalization-the-new-era-of-global-flows>

[88] De Tijd June 7 2016 Chinese koopwoede op recordhoogte

[89] De Tijd – 7 November 2015 De Nieuwe Tijden

[90] https://www.youtube.com/watch?v=QFrqTFRy-LU

[91] http://100people.org/statistics_detailed_statistics.php

[92] https://www.cia.gov/library/publications/the-world-factbook/

[93] http://www.fastcompany.com/3056737/fast-feed/alphabets-project-loon-to-begin-delivering-internet-access-this-year

[94] http://www.usatoday.com/story/experience/2016/05/26/microsoft-facebook-undersea-cable-google-marea-amazon/84984882/

[95] http://www.forbes.com/sites/valleyvoices/2015/03/13/which-industries-are-uber-vulnerable-for-cloud-disruption/#7f636161720e

[96] http://www.slideshare.net/EmergenceCapital/industry-cloud-forum-emergence-capital-keynote

[97] De Tijd – May 13 2016 – Einde musicdownload nakend

[98] www.swift.com/insights/news/the-chinese-road-to-platform-disruption

[99] http://www.pv-tech.org/features/20-energy-storage-disruptors

[100] Agoria Energiewende

[101] http://singularityhub.com/2016/03/16/stay-ahead-of-the-next-industrial-revolution-with-exponential-manufacturing/

[102] De Tijd June 4 CEO behave like politicians

[103] Digitaal geheugenverlies: hoe smartphones ons geheugen overnemen, Door Nathalie van Raemdonck, 7 September 2015

[104] https://kasperskycontenthub.com/usa/files/2015/06/Digital-Amnesia-Report.pdf

[105] http://www.dailymail.co.uk/sciencetech/article-3618467/The-teenage-brain-social-media-Scans-reveal-liking-post-activates-circuits-eating-chocolate-winning-money.html

[106] Bain Brand Accelerator – Guest Lecture UGent April 2015

[107] http://www.informationisbeautiful.net/visualizations/worlds-biggest-data-breaches-hacks/

[108] https://www.pwc.com/gx/en/industries/industry-4.0.html

[109] http://www.oxfordmartin.ox.ac.uk

[110] http://www.oxfordmartin.ox.ac.uk/publications/view/1883

[111] http://www.theatlantic.com/magazine/archive/2015/07/world-without-work/395294/

[112] https://www.weforum.org/reports/the-future-of-jobs

[113] http://www.newequipment.com/Main/topstories/Chinas-Factories-Go-Dark-as-Robots-Take-Over-1429.aspx

[114] http://i4j.info/2016/03/is-unemployment-a-problem-or-an-opportunity/

[115] http://www.modis.com/it-insights/infographics/top-it-jobs-of-2016/

[116] Gazet Van Antwerpen May 29 2016 AI

[117] http://www.robovalley.com/

[118] http://www.csiro.au/en/Research/D61/Areas/Data-for-decisions/Strategic-Foresight/Tomorrows-Digitally-Enabled-Workforce

[119] https://www.weforum.org/agenda/2016/02/these-scientists-have-predicted-which-jobs-will-be-human-only-in-2035/

[120] https://www.washingtonpost.com/posteverything/wp/2016/02/17/yes-the-robots-will-steal-our-jobs-and-thats-fine/

[121] https://www.weforum.org/agenda/2016/06/8-digital-skills-we-must-teach-our-children/

[122] http://www.mckinsey.com/business-functions/business-technology/our-insights/how-to-get-the-most-from-big-data

[123] http://digital2020.be/industry-4-0-threat-or-opportunity/

[124] http://www.wired.com/2015/08/robots-will-steal-jobs-theyll-give-us-new-ones/

Energise Your Way Forward

[125] Check out Adam Curtis's video series on The Century Of Me

[126] http://robertwaldinger.com/

[127] https://www.youtube.com/watch?v=lYdNjrUs4NM

[128] www.jimcollins.com/article_topics/articles/secret-of-enduring-greatness.html

[129] http://www.lynda.com/Business-Skills-tutorials/Disrupting-Yourself/153829-2.html

[130] http://www.attendly.com/john-cleese-on-creativity-and-how-to-unleash-your-tortoise-brain/

[131] http://www.carminegallo.com/

[132] http://www.vault.com/company-rankings/consulting/best-consulting-firms-prestige

[133] https://www.weforum.org/agenda/2016/03/could-this-simple-trick-make-you-more-creative

[134] http://martinprosperity.org/content/the-global-creativity-index-2015/

[135] http://www.eweek.com/small-business/businesses-struggle-to-implement-digital-transformation.html

[136] http://www.mckinsey.com/business-functions/operations/our-insights/how-to-scale-your-own-digital-disruption

[137] http://www.strategy-business.com/article/Your-Next-Board-Member-Should-Be-a-Geek?gko=7758e

[138] http://fundersandfounders.com/aha-moments-for-entrepreneurs/